How a city is born, grows, decays, and is renewed is explored through the story of three city neighborhoods. These communities are in New York City but their problems are typical of city neighborhoods throughout the country. As the reader is introduced to each neighborhood's past and present growth, and the people who live and work in each area, these places become real, even to those unfamiliar with them. And each of the areas—Chelsea, Coney Island, and Jamaica—has a different combination of forces at work shaping its future.

What makes a neighborhood a better place to live: improved housing, community controlled change, increased employment opportunities? What roles do federal, state, and city government play? How do private developers and organized groups of citizens help shape the community?

Block by Block deals with many such questions in an absorbing manner. And, beyond this, it considers the important question of whether individuals, young and old, can effectively improve their environment when that environment is a small part of a complex metropolis.

BLOCK BY BLOCK

Rebuilding City Neighborhoods

Martha E. Munzer &

Helen W. Vogel

Alfred A. Knopf / New York

To Ginny, Johnny and Tom—
builders of the future.

THIS IS A BORZOI BOOK PUBLISHED BY ALFRED A. KNOPF, INC.

Copyright © 1973 by *Martha E. Munzer & Helen W. Vogel.* All rights reserved under International and Pan-American Copyright Conventions. Published in the United States by Alfred A. Knopf, Inc., New York, and simultaneously in Canada by Random House of Canada Limited, Toronto. Distributed by Random House, Inc., New York. Designed by Elliot Epstein. Manufactured in the United States of America.

Library of Congress Cataloging in Publication Data

Munzer, Martha E. Block by block.

Summary: Using New York as an example, traces the birth, growth, decay, and renewal of a city.

1. New York (City)—Social conditions—Juvenile literature. [1. New York (City)—Social conditions. 2. Cities and towns] I. Vogel, Helen Wolff, joint author. II. Title. HN80.N5M85 309.1'747'1 73-5780 ISBN 0-394-82132-7 ISBN 0-394-92132-1 (lib. ed.)

Acknowledgments

The assistance of many generous people made possible the writing and publication of this book.

One of our first tasks was the selection of specific neighborhoods from among a number of possibilities. For wise counsel in the making of initial choices we are indebted to Professor George Raymond, city planner and faculty member of the New School for Social Research; Roger Starr, Executive Director of the City Housing and Planning Council; and Alex Cooper of New York's Department of City Planning.

For ongoing help with the Chelsea story we owe special thanks to H. Daniel Carpenter, Executive Director of the Hudson Guild; Don Martin, Secretary of the United Housing Foundation; and Bruce Buckley, Editor of the *Chelsea Clinton News,* and his wife, Joan.

For assistance in creating the section on Coney Island we wish to thank Marcey Feigenbaum in the office of the Brooklyn Borough President; Nell Miller, Librarian of the John Dewey High School; community leaders Sophie Smith and Gloria Edwards; Doris Hart of the Urban Task Force; Celia Kushner of the Community Planning Board; Donald Trump, developer and builder; and Walter Fass, board member of Luna Park Houses.

And for assistance with the Jamaica story our thanks are extended to Robert Friedrich of the Queensborough Public Library; F. Carlisle Towery and Helen A. Levine of the Greater Jamaica Development Corporation; David Starr, Editor of the *Long Island Press;* Richard A. White of the Jamaica Chamber of Commerce; and John Palm of the National Bank of North America.

To Miss Charlotte LaRue, of the Museum of the City of New York, and Mr. Val Coleman, of the New York City Housing Authority, our warm thanks for their help in finding a number of our book's illustrations.

To our numerous hosts and acquaintances in each of the neighborhoods, our appreciation for the warmth of their welcome and the generosity of their help. Many of these people are introduced by name in the text itself. A few had to be omitted because there just wasn't room. There are some whose names we never learned. To all we offer this general but nonetheless genuine thank you.

A special word of appreciation goes to Laurence Orton, member emeritus of the New York City Planning Commission, who not only directed us to Jamaica, but who also read the completed manuscript with critical acumen and professional skill.

An oft-repeated thank you goes to our friend Dr. Nancy Ziebur for her thoughtful and perceptive suggestions on the entire text, and to Virginia Fowler for her faith in the book and her contributions to it.

For her patient, efficient typing, retyping and re-retyping of the manuscript we owe gratitude to Mrs. John Secco.

As to our Editors, without whose creative partnership *Block by Block* would never have been put between covers, thank you is an all too inadequate way of conveying our appreciation.

Grateful acknowledgment is made for permission to use the following illustrations:

Chelsea Clinton News, 3, 7, 13, 15, 23, 27, 41, 55, 59, 63, 69; New York Public Library Picture Collection, 18, 77, 84; Photography by Bryon, The Bryon Collection, Museum of the City of New York, 21, 82; Museum of the City of New York, 26, 74, 78, 80; Hudson Guild, 30, 38, 67; New York City Housing Authority, 32, 36, 44, 90, 98; The Society for Ethical Culture in the City of New York, 34; United Housing Foundation, Sam Reiss Photographer, 50; United Housing Foundation, 51; Wendy Holmes, Wave Hill Center for Environmental Studies, 61; The Trump Organization, 94; Arne Aakre, 102, 107; Long Island Division, Queens Borough Public Library, 112; *Long Island Press,* 114, 119, 127, 129; Jamaica Chamber of Commerce, 118, 122, 124, 132, 137; Photography by Wilson, 163–18 Jamaica Avenue, New York, 141; City University of New York, 147.

Martha E. Munzer
Helen W. Vogel

Contents

BLOCK BY BLOCK

Introduction
THE BLOCK YOU LIVE ON

It was a bloody battle. Before the street fighting was over, seven people had been arrested, thirty more had been injured, and two were dead.

This riot took place in a New York City ghetto on a sweltering night in the summer of 1967. The inhabitants of East Harlem were filled with bitterness, frustration, and hatred of a world over which they had no control. Cooped up in poverty and misery, the people vented their feelings on the hot slums which were their prison.

The rumored shooting of a Puerto Rican had triggered this wild night of fighting between the police (la jarra) and the hot, resentful people bursting out of their steamy tenements.

Mobs of teenagers exploded into the garbage filled streets, smashing a third of the windows in the neighborhood. A thousand police were sent to the scene and were at once pelted with a shower of bottles hurled by young and old alike.

An eyewitness described what happened next: "A mob of rioters, looting, burning, was surging down Third Avenue and headed for East 100th Street, bent on destruction. As they approached, a barricade of men formed at the entrance to the block. Scores of other people stood behind them on the street and sidewalk. These local leaders told the band of rioters to get out. 'Don't come down our block.' After a moment's hesitation and a quick glance at the men opposing them they turned and fled. The block remained unscathed."

Why did the people of East 100th Street, often called "the city's worst block," choose to defend it? It was a neighborhood with a multitude of problems—narcotics traffic, burglaries, bad housing—the ills of poor neighborhoods throughout our country.

In ghettos like this, in cities across the United States, despair and hopelessness have moved people to destroy, not to protect, their neighborhoods. Burning down cities—this was the response of the poor to their anger and frustration in the 1960's.

But what made the people of East 100th Street respond in such a different way? Norman Eddy, a resident of the East Harlem area, explains his neighbors' choice to defend rather than destroy their block: "Behind this minor incident lies the history of a poor neighborhood which has been determined to rebuild itself physically and spiritually, under its own leadership, with its own plans, and developing its own power to get them executed."

The residents of East 100th Street had for some time been working for needed change in an organized way. They were beginning to carry out plans for their neighborhood, plans which they themselves had drawn up. Some deteriorated housing was in the process of being remodeled for the families who lived on the street. City agencies and private charitable foundations were supplying needed funds. In addition, the City Government had adopted a program to build new, low-income housing projects. One such development was slated to rise on a junk-filled lot in the area. To harness the energies of the young people, a group of teenagers had formed a neighborhood club. Their programs included exciting new recreational activities and an ongoing effort to stem the tide of drug addiction among their peers. The people of East 100th Street,

Cleaning up the neighborhood—block by block.

young and old, had a commitment to each other and to the block they lived on.

Young people in many places are playing an active part in rebuilding their communities. Houses have been brightened with fresh paint, sagging doors replaced, and railings repaired. Vacant, rubbish filled lots have been cleaned out and turned into small playgrounds or vest pocket parks.

A specific example of such concern and action is found in a blighted section of New York City's South Bronx. A group of twenty-four high school and college students united and formed a group called Students for Progress in the Community (S.P.I.C.). The first job they set for themselves was the clean-up of a small area in one of the busiest sections of the neighborhood.

This is how they described their initial activity of May 27, 1972:

> Today, for most of us, is our first visit to Crane Square. . . . On this warm, sunny morning we are greeted by garbage cans strewn about the ground, on fire, and others hopelessly battered.
>
> Newspapers cover the ground along with broken whiskey bottles, empty glue tubes, food and winos. . . .
>
> . . . The Square needs cleaning badly and it seems that, if we don't do it, nobody will. For most of us, the Square is right by our homes, so it seems the logical place to begin. Our plans are to paint the subway stations, newstands and benches. Two of the benches are in need of repair and we hope to take care of that too. There are also plans to paint hop-scotch and various other children's games on the pavement, and to request restoration of the restrooms by the Parks Department. One of our art students has offered to paint a mural on the outside of the restrooms. But our greatest goal is to set up a community bulletin board so that residents can learn of cultural events and health and educational programs.
>
> These are very high goals for us considering our total lack of

funds. The only money and equipment available to us is our own small savings and a few brooms contributed by the Bronx Environmental Society Inc. (another teenage organization). . . .

We began our first day by sweeping up the garbage. We developed headaches, backaches, blisters, but with that, a sense of satisfaction for having begun a worthwhile task . . .

There was not much more we could do that first afternoon. We had finished sweeping up the litter from the ground, deposited it in the garbage cans, and collected aluminum cans and bottles for a nearby recycling center . . .

The final clean-ups were spent on maintaining the cleanness of the park. . . . The important thing now seems to be the response of the people living in the area. They seem to be more careful about throwing garbage in the park and have even developed a new respect for their park.

For S.P.I.C., this is the desired result of a clean-up, to make people realize that a park is theirs to enjoy as well as to keep clean.

A sprucing up, or face-lifting job, important as it may be, is only a small part of the work that needs to be done if our cities are to be rebuilt as fit places in which to live.

A high school class in Miami, Florida concentrated on another facet of the task. The students decided to take a close look at their neighborhood to see how the needs of the people living there were being met. They discovered that because their community had grown by sprawling outward instead of developing around a core, it lacked a focal point. What was needed, they decided, was a community center to bring people together. Such a center, they agreed, would provide adults, teenagers, and younger children with new opportunities for active group participation.

First there were many questions to be answered. Did the residents want such a center? If so, what did they wish it to contain? Once this information was obtained, it would be necessary to make a survey of the facilities already available in the community.

Where might the center be located? To answer this question, available sites would have to be explored. What architectural design would be most suitable for the selected tract of land? Here professional help would be needed. And finally, the students would have to figure the approximate cost of the center, and find out how such an undertaking could be financed.

The young people proceeded to draw up a questionnaire and submitted it to a scientifically selected sample of the community, for reactions and suggestions. The researchers were soon armed with a favorable response to the idea, and an understanding of what their neighbors wanted the center to contain. There was need for an auditorium, a library, and recreation rooms for both noisy and quiet games. In addition, the people polled wanted a swimming pool, athletic courts, and a playground. It was also suggested that the center include a restaurant which could help defray some of the running expenses of the other facilities.

The next step was to find a site. The students located a strip of county owned land adjoining a nearby public park. Then came consultations with a local architect, a contractor, a banker, and a city official. Finally, a three-dimensional model including floor plans and landscaping design was constructed.

A professional version of the proposed center may perhaps be built some day. As of now, a great many adults have been alerted to the desirability of a community facility and the possibility of its creation. To bring the center into being, the entire neighborhood will need to work together to persuade the City Government to back the project and take the necessary steps for its creation.

The students gained an awareness of their neighborhood's

Young people dig for a greener neighborhood.

needs and learned something about what it takes to meet those needs. They encountered some of the problems of people and politics that have to be solved before dreams can become realities.

These young people began to acquaint themselves with, and use, the tools that will enable them to become creative and effective agents of change. In fact, their initial effort, the community center, may some day be more than a blueprint!

Young people can play a constructive part in rebuilding neighborhoods, as we have seen in New York and Miami. The same thing is happening in many other communities. Is it taking place in yours?

How about your immediate neighborhood—your own block? Would you work to save it? Does it satisfactorily fulfill the needs of your friends and family? What changes would you like to see? Would you work for these improvements?

How did your neighborhood become the way it is today? Usually, homes are built, and neighborhoods develop around them. As the houses get older they deteriorate and people who can afford it, move away and live farther out. Birth—growth—decay; neighborhoods are like people.

But a neighborhood's life doesn't *have* to end that way. Sometimes a community rises from its own ashes. We can learn why and how this happens by taking a close look at city areas that have reversed the process of decay.

The three neighborhoods we will examine with you are in New York City. Their stories illustrate a number of different approaches to neighborhood renewal. Though the areas we studied have their own unique features and history, they are also prototypes of blighted areas in almost any city, and very likely in your own.

The study of the life cycles of these selected neighborhoods, and the dramatic story of their rebirth, will give you insights into the possible ways in which you can help to revitalize your own block and neighborhood, your own city, town, or suburb.

Let us start by venturing into an old community on mid-Manhattan's West Side. The area is known as Chelsea. Some of those who have lived there for a long time remember when a corner of it was called by a saltier name—"Hell's Kitchen."

PART ONE

CHELSEA

A Tough Neighborhood Turns Around

A Walk Through Chelsea

"A patchwork of town houses, tenements, factories and housing projects"—this is the way the American Institute of Architects, in its *Guide to New York City*, describes the area known
as Chelsea. It is an apt description of the neighborhood, with
its blackened warehouses sandwiched between decaying four
and five story rooming houses and its neat, newly renovated
row houses overshadowed by tall apartment buildings. The
latter range from the austere, unadorned slabs of public
housing developments to one of the world's most massive
apartment complexes, London Terrace, whose doormen, cos-
tumed as London "bobbies," add an engaging touch of British
color.

To get the feel of Chelsea one should take a leisurely walk
through its streets—streets that combine an aura of the past
with a sense of the aliveness of the present.

Markers sunk into sidewalks or embedded in walls, tell of
past glories—the site of an old Opera House or a long vanished
theater.

Plaques, such as the one affixed to a beautiful group of
town houses called Cushman Row, identify historic buildings.

These red brick four story homes are graced with fanciful iron balustrades on stairs leading up to deeply recessed doorways framed in brownstone. Living vines reach up to small attic windows decorated with stone-carved wreaths. The plaque tells us that these handsome houses were built in 1840 by Don Alonzo Cushman, parish leader and financier.

Chelsea has other examples of this architectural style known, because of its use of classic Greek detail, as Greek Revival. Some of the houses are abandoned and boarded up, the brownstone cornices crumbling, the iron railings broken. Others, also in dilapidated condition, are alive with roomers. A number are in the process of restoration, while still others appear to have retained their original beauty.

Chelsea is first and foremost a *people* place. And the people we see on our first ramble impress us as being a mixed group. Though most of the inhabitants are white, there are many black, tan, and brown people living in Chelsea. The young people could be the young of any neighborhood, in any city, dressed as they are in blue jeans and pullovers. The older people range in costume from the conservatively well-dressed to the shabbily clothed.

The pace is leisurely; most people seem to be enjoying the mellow light of this late fall afternoon. The general atmosphere is one of warmth and friendliness.

There is, for example, the old janitor who graciously unlocks the door of a church with a name that intrigues us. Church of the Guardian Angel—Shrine Church of the Sea, reminds us that Chelsea borders the waterfront, though there is no way to get a glimpse of the Hudson from the street. Tall warehouses and railroad buildings, gigantic piers and an overhead highway, completely block the view.

Across from the church is a small, tree shaded area, called Clement Moore Park. Several groups of men are engrossed in chess or checkers; mothers are chatting with each other while

Greek Revival architecture in Chelsea.

rocking baby carriages; youngsters of assorted ages are playing hide-and-seek in the shrubbery.

On a wall that abuts the park is a large poster decorated
with brightly painted tulips. The poster bears this inscription:

Let the 2000 flowers bloom.
Explain to others, bulbs and
  shoots must be left alone
  so they can become flowers.
If you take one home only
  you will see it.
Let everyone see flowers
  in your park.

A boy is standing nearby, "Do you know who made that
poster?" we ask.

"You bet I do," is his quick reply. "*We* did, in my class in the
school across the street." There is a note of pride in his voice.

Several blocks away we enter another small open area—
this a dismal one. It is part of the open space provided for the
people who live in one of Chelsea's low-income housing
projects. There seems to be no proper play area for children in
this section because most of the available space has nothing in
it except some long, drab benches. The layout is not even
conducive to pleasant relaxation. "Suicide Alley is what we call
it," remarks an elderly black man with whom we sit for a few
moments.

Several teenagers are huddled together on one of the
benches. Rather shyly they tell us that for them, too, Chelsea
holds no lure. "Nothing really to do," "We're scared to go out,"
"And we're scared inside the housing project, too."

Leaving the so-called park, we stroll back along Ninth
Avenue and come upon a store whose name tempts us to enter.
"Price-less Salvage" is a menagerie of bric-a-brac, old clocks,
kitchen utensils, and ancient household furnishings.

Clement Moore Park.

After browsing a while we exchange introductions with the proprietor, Valdis Kupris. On learning of our mission, he immediately invites us to take a look at his recently restored town house around the corner. Being an artist and craftsman, Mr. Kupris has used his skill to transform a decrepit old rooming house into a charming and original home, studio, and gallery.

"I and my family wouldn't want to live in a better place than Chelsea," he comments. "It's great!"

As we are about to leave the tree-shaded row of houses, we see a young woman sitting on one of the stoops. We fall into conversation. She has just returned from her job in a publishing house and is relaxing for a few moments before climbing to her apartment on the top floor.

Chelsea was her first choice for living. "It's so convenient to my work and to all the other places I want to go. But, what's more important, it's such an exciting and friendly neighborhood. Summer evenings it's like a fiesta, with all kinds of people sitting on their steps, singing and strumming guitars."

Her final comment is this: "As a rule, a person can't put down roots through concrete, but it seems that's exactly what I've done."

Flashback

But what was it like in the Chelsea area before roots had to push their way through concrete?

Let us go back in time, like a movie film in reverse, erasing the modern image of a city neighborhood. Our camera zooms into focus on a river-bordered wilderness of wooded glades and streams, with hills rising gently from the shore. A few Indians are hunting and fishing. This is the unnamed Chelsea of the early 1600's, when the Dutch first started their settlement some two and a half miles to the south, at the foot of the island.

A century passes. New Amsterdam has become New York. The harbor and port are flourishing, bringing not only trade but thousands of newcomers from the Old World. The town becomes more and more congested and the prosperous people begin to push their way in the only available direction—ever farther and farther to the north on narrow, elongated Manhattan Island.

The western area above Fourteenth Street, the future Chelsea, is still wilderness except for a single tobacco plantation. Then in 1750, a ninety-four acre tract of this hinterland is purchased by a retired British Army Captain, Thomas Clarke. Wanting to escape the crowded, noisy city, the Captain builds himself and his family a sturdy frame farmhouse. In a mood of nostalgia he names it Chelsea House in honor of Chelsea Royal Hospital, a famous home for retired soldiers near London.

Thus the story of New York's Chelsea—today's concrete-covered Chelsea—begins.

Clarke's grandson, Clement Clarke Moore (who is still remembered and memorialized for his verse "'Twas the Night Before Christmas") eventually fell heir to his grandfather's estate. He loved his rural acres and wanted to keep them intact. But his desire was soon overridden.

Because the city was pushing outward in a helter-skelter fashion, the State Legislature, in 1807, appointed a commission headed by John R. Randall Jr., to draw up suitable plans for the orderly growth of the city. The commissioners decided on a crisscrossing, today called a gridiron pattern, because "a city is to be composed principally of the habitations of men . . . and straight sided and right angled houses are the most cheap to build and the most convenient to live in."

Natural beauty was given no value by the hard-headed businessmen who ruled New York when the Randall Commission set to work. Under the plan that evolved, no effort was

The Moore mansion, 1854.

made to take advantage of the natural features of the island; its streams and hills, its trees and valleys.

To Clement Moore, the edict compelling conformity to the new, rigid pattern of streets and avenues meant the cutting up and leveling of his lovely rural acres. Wistfully he remarked, "When the streets and avenues about Chelsea were regulated, it was thought advisable, if not absolutely necessary, to dig down the whole place and throw it into the river."

Bowing finally to the inevitability of the city's encroachment on the countryside, Moore decided to break up his property. He gave a large rectangular part of his farmland, a section of his apple orchard, to the General Theological Seminary of the Protestant Episcopal Church.

Prosperous people from the heart of downtown, who could drive out to the country in their carriages, were soon buying lots and building town houses on various portions of Moore's property. Most valued was Chelsea Square around the Seminary. The prosperous Don Alonzo Cushman built his "Row" facing the red brick walls of the "minister factory," as the institution was dubbed by a local wit.

Another gentleman of wealth chose Twenty-third Street, the main thoroughfare, on which to build a series of elegant townhouses. They were promptly referred to as "Millionaire's Row." By the mid-nineteenth century the entire area had become a fashionable community. It was known as Chelsea Village.

Still there was pressure to expand, so the city fathers decided to create more land by filling the marshes along the Hudson. The crisscrossing continued and three new avenues were added as north-south arteries, intersected by freshly created east-west streets.

Thus the suburban village kept growing in its rigid gridiron pattern until it was completely merged with the ever-expanding city. It's character, however, was so firmly established, that to this day Chelsea has its own invisible borders—Fourteenth to Thirtieth Streets south to north, and Sixth Avenue—Avenue of the Americas—to the river, six long crosstown blocks east to west.

Almost all of our American cities have developed in much this way. The gridiron pattern of streets and avenues pushes the city outward from its center, finally engulfing the outlying villages. Many of these smaller units have retained something of their original flavor, no longer as country villages but rather as city neighborhoods.

In the decades just before the turn of the century, old Chelsea presented a panorama of handsome cabs, victorias, surreys, gentlemen with sideburns, and ladies with parasols. Lively couples stopped at Cavanagh's on Twenty-third Street for shell-fish and a glass of sherry, and then continued down the block to the Grand Opera House owned by two officers of the Erie Railroad, Jim Fisk and Jay Gould.

Many of the famous actresses and writers of the day—Sarah Bernhardt, Lillian Russell, Mark Twain, O. Henry—resided at the Chelsea Hotel on Twenty-third Street. This unique hotel, with its balconies trimmed in iron scrollwork and its wide, curved stairway inside, became one of Chelsea's proudest landmarks.

Change and Decay

Despite the glitter and gaiety of the fashionable Chelsea of the late nineteenth century, seeds of decay were already planted and beginning to sprout. Ironically, the trouble sprang largely from one of the city's most valuable assets, its incomparable harbor, which at all seasons provided safe and abundant docking facilities for overseas trade and transportation.

First came the sailing vessels, carrying their cargoes to and

Chelsea's busy waterfront, 1896.

from Manhattan's harbor. As the age of sail gave way to the age of steam, larger and larger ships, both passenger and merchant, found anchorage along the shoreline of lower and mid-Manhattan. Presently, Chelsea's waterfront was completely covered with piers, wharves, and bulkheads constructed on the filled-in mud flats.

In 1847, following on the heels of the increasing maritime activity, Commodore Vanderbilt's Hudson River Railroad started to lay its tracks close to the city's shoreline. Thus cargo could easily be transferred from ships to freight cars heading out of the city toward the West.

Along with the railroad came industry which needed to be near heavy duty long distance transportation. And so the western part of Chelsea was gradually disfigured with brickyards, lumberyards, gas works, slaughterhouses, iron works, distilleries, warehouses, and freightyards. Shabby homes for the laborers were squeezed in between the industry.

The new railroad, with a franchise from the city, was permitted to run its tracks right down the centers of Tenth and Eleventh Avenues. As a result, the streets and houses became blanketed with smoke and cinders from the puffing, noisy, wood-fired locomotives. The locomotives were preceded by an advance guard of "Death Avenue Cowboys" on horseback, waving bright red flags of warning.

Soon the blighted neighborhood was darkened still further by the construction of an overhead transit system, the Ninth Avenue El. The overhead railway, though useful as a means of rapid transit, could not help but add to the noise, dirt, and ugliness of western Chelsea. And the blight kept slowly spreading, from the banks of the Hudson eastward, until it touched the fringes of the millionaires' rows. It became increasingly clear that the neighborhood's few short years of preeminence as a fashionable center were fast drawing to a close.

Householders were dismayed, and those with the means to

Ninth Avenue - at W. 29th St.

Rapid transportation at the turn of the century—the Ninth Avenue el.

do so began to pull out and locate farther uptown. As the rich moved out of their elegant town houses, middle-class people moved in. And then, as the neighborhood continued to deteriorate, they also took flight. The poor, who had crowded into Chelsea to help turn "the wheels of progress," had no such option. They had to remain. And they crowded into the old dwellings which were transformed into rooming houses. Now there were more and more people jammed into less and less space. The harder use of the buildings accelerated their decay. Landlords, in search of profits, made fewer and fewer repairs. The houses deteriorated still further. Urban blight, in the shape of a slum, was slowly and inexorably created.

This pattern of growth and decay has followed the same sad sequence in many cities across our land. A neighborhood of wealthy landowners in a previously rural area, the creeping up of industry, a population explosion of the poor seeking work and shelter, the flight of the rich, the eventual abandonment of the area to the powerless—you inescapably end up with a slum.

The blight that infected Chelsea also infected the lives of the people who were trapped in its confines. Most of these people had come from Europe, immigrants of many nationalities—the French, Spanish, Italians, Germans, Greeks, and in greatest number the Irish—all filled with high hopes for a better life. Many labored as seamen, porters, factory hands, or drivers of trucking wagons. Still others worked as longshoremen (short for along-the-shore men).

The women were also needed as wage-earners to supply even the meagerest living for their families. With the men they shared the miserable employment conditions—the long hours in sweatshops, the starvation pay—offered in the garment industry, fast growing in that part of the city. Many of the women with small children brought home mountainous piles of piecework from the clothing factories. Home, for the immigrant laboring people, was a room or two in a dilapidated rooming house, or in a hastily built tenement.

Fights quickly developed among the different ethnic groups. Street gangs, already traditional in New York, sprang up in Chelsea. The most notorious of these were the Hudson River Dusters, the Gophers, and the Tenth Avenue Gang.

The rough boys from these gangs, so the legend goes, used to congregate at a combination beer saloon and restaurant located somewhere in the northwest corner of Chelsea. The place was run by a husband and wife called Heil. To the door they had affixed a sign reading "Heil's Kitchen."

When the gang members got hungry for pig's knuckles and sauerkraut, or thirsty for large glasses of foaming beer, they would call out to each other, "Let's go down to Hell's Kitchen." Whether the mispronunciation was innocent or deliberate, the neighborhood, which extended north beyond Chelsea into Clinton, became known as Hell's Kitchen.

The name was indeed appropriate, for this and other sections of Chelsea had become scenes of vice, crime, and corruption, involving people from the top to the bottom of the economic scale, from exploiters to exploited, from corrupters to corrupted.

An oldtimer, revisiting the Chelsea of memory, might well have echoed the words of a popular hymn of the time: "Change and decay in all around I see."

Man with a Mission

It was on a crisp fall day in 1894, that a tall, mustached young man was walking through those changed and decayed streets of Chelsea. He was immediately struck by the dismal, soot-covered tenements where people lived surrounded by slaughterhouses and stables.

The stroller, John Lovejoy Elliott, was a mid-westerner from the farming community of Princeton, Illinois. His father had commanded a regiment in the Civil War; his mother was related

Outdoor living—city style, then . . .

And now.

to Elijah Lovejoy, the slain Abolitionist theologian and editor. Both parents had played an active part in helping southern blacks escape to freedom. This was the heritage of the young man who had come east to attend college at Cornell. While there he had met a scholar who was to influence the entire course of his life, and, indirectly, the lives of many others.

Professor Felix Adler, originally trained as a rabbi, had in 1876 established the Society for Ethical Culture in New York City. This small group of religious humanists expressed the faith that men were capable of improving society through their own efforts without Divine intervention.

John Elliott joined the Ethical Culture movement under Professor Adler's leadership. The young idealist began at once to look for the specific line of action that would capture his imagination and harness his energies, for "Deed not Creed" was one of the guiding principles of the society.

The deed which he searched for was waiting for him as he wandered through the streets of Chelsea on that fine autumn day. On a sidewalk on West Twenty-sixth Street he noticed a group of men, not much younger than he, shooting craps.

"You know fellows," John Elliott is said to have remarked, "It's against the law to shoot craps in the street. What do you say we go inside where the police won't bother us?"

With the support of his uptown friends from the Ethical Society, he rented a room and issued an invitation to the young men of Chelsea to visit the new clubhouse. A mere handful arrived, and if it hadn't been for a set of boxing gloves which Dr. Elliott happened to have with him, the meeting might well have led nowhere. The newly organized club, The Hurley Burlies, survived and grew. Other clubs were added. Song-fests were initiated and boisterous renditions of such popular favorites as "The Sidewalks of New York" and "After the Ball Was Over" were given.

Dr. Elliott recalled in later years that a local minister

reported the organization to the police as "a menace to neighborhood morality," which it was not, and "a disturber of the peace," which it was.

The "disturber of the peace" continued to flourish. Presently, in 1908, it developed into a settlement house—The Hudson Guild—with its own five story brick building on Twenty-seventh Street, between Ninth and Tenth Avenues, in the heart of Chelsea.

Settlement houses were not new to the City of New York; in fact, the first one to be established in America had opened its doors on the Lower East Side in 1886 as the Neighborhood Guild—later to be known as the University Settlement. The year 1894 marked the birth of Henry Street Settlement in lower Manhattan.

These early settlement houses were designed to fill a vital need of the poverty-stricken immigrants who were swarming to our shores. It was the function of the settlements to provide urgently needed havens of warmth and friendliness in a city filled with strangers.

At the Hudson Guild, the original young men's athletic club was soon one among many groups including a mothers' club, a day care center for children below school age, and a school for printers. There was something for *everyone*—cooking, sewing, carpentry, sports, square dancing, and drama. These classes and recreational activities not only aided people in learning skills, but also provided Chelsea's mixed ethnic population with an exciting social center where neighbors were quick to learn to help themselves and each other.

Most of the financial and moral support continued to come through the successful efforts of members and friends of the Ethical Society. Dr. Elliott, who taught Ethics at the society's uptown school, encouraged his students (the senior author of this book among them) to prepare food baskets at Thanksgiving, Christmas, and Easter time for distribution to those whose

Chelsea's own settlement house—the original Hudson Guild.

cupboards were bare. He inspired some among us to journey down to the Hudson Guild after school to lend a hand in the various activities. John Elliott was the kind of man who, through his enthusiasm and example, could and did activate others.

From the early days of the guild, John Elliott had identified himself with the poor of Chelsea by living among them in a tenement flat. In this way he learned first hand of the intolerable conditions under which many of his neighbors lived: the leaky roofs, the filth, the stench, the disorder, the crowding.

The city, prodded by the guild to investigate, discovered that almost half of Chelsea's tenement house apartments—dwellings occupied by the poor—lacked central heat. About a third of them had no hot water, no tub or shower, no private toilet. Such "cold water flats" existed not only in Chelsea but in many other areas throughout the city, and in most other large cities as well.

Through the guild's initiative, district committees were organized. One person was designated captain of each block in the district and had a supporting group of neighbors whose duty it was to report and help solve such problems as lack of food or fuel, unsanitary building conditions, threats of eviction, and needs for medical care. Those were the days long before such services as social security, unemployment insurance, welfare, and medicare existed.

Through the kind of "people power" encouraged by the guild, things started to happen: a clean-up of Chelsea Park; the erection of a public bathhouse on Twenty-eighth Street; the demolition of some Twenty-sixth Street buildings known graphically and accurately as "Bedbug Row." These improvements were pitifully small in terms of the total need for change. But at least there was less rubbish in the streets, a little more paint on decrepit buildings, several new stores, and a few more factories or offices in place of vacant lots.

"Home" in a city tenement.

A "model tenement" was completed on Twenty-eighth Street in the early 1920's, thanks to the organized efforts of the supporters of Hudson Guild. The revolutionary feature of the thirty-four apartment, six story building called Chelsea Homes was a private bath for each living unit.

Neighborhood reaction to this innovation was sadly ironic. One housewife, upon hearing that each flat would have its own toilet, exclaimed, "What! We got to have one of them smelly things in our house?"

But small efforts, such as Chelsea Homes, supported by civic-minded individual philanthropists, did not begin to touch the real need—a massive supply of decent low-rent housing for the neighborhood.

Housing for the poor had been, for some time, one of the most vexing problems in Chelsea. Enforcement of new laws made miserable tenements a bit more sanitary, but they still remained unfit for decent living. Dr. Elliott and people like him—a small minority—were declaring that providing adequate housing was as much a responsibility of government as was furnishing public schools or supplying water. This was indeed a revolutionary idea. And it took a number of years, much hard politicking on the part of many ordinary citizens, plus a great depression, to bring Congress around.

A changed point of view finally led to the passage of the Housing Act of 1937, the first permanent housing program in our nation's history subsidized by the Federal Government. In the act's preamble, Congress declared that the shortage of decent dwellings for families whose incomes were so low that private industry could not meet their needs was "injurious to the nation" and that the provision of housing for this group was a federal responsibility. The act also declared the elimination of slums to be a national goal. To make a start, federal loans and subsidies were provided to help cities erect housing for their low-income families.

Chelsea's number one good neighbor, John L. Elliott.

Hudson Guild members lost not a moment's time after the passage of the act. Under Dr. Elliott's leadership, they helped to organize the Chelsea Association for Planning and Action (CAPA). The group took as its top priority decent housing, at prices that could be afforded by the people who needed it most. The first task of the new organization was to convince the New York City Housing Authority, whose funds came from local as well as federal sources, that there should be a project in Chelsea. The plan presented called for the housing of 617 of Chelsea's low-income families. The authority gave a dozen reasons why this could not be, with most of the arguments boiling down to a question of cost. Undaunted, CAPA found a group of decrepit buildings adjacent to the Hudson Guild Neighborhood House, that could be bought quite cheaply. The Chelsea organization presented its case so effectively that the housing project finally received official approval.

In 1941, the condemned tenements were razed in preparation for the new housing project. Then, quite suddenly, all action was suspended as national and local priorities shifted to wartime demands. In 1945 Mayor Fiorello La Guardia finally turned the first spadeful of earth for the John L. Elliott Houses, but the man for whom they were named was no longer there to know. He had died in 1942.

John Elliott never reached the "Promised Land" of his dreams—a land that offered, among many other things, living space fit for people. He never viewed the four, red brick buildings that rose eleven and twelve stories high, replacing dank, dark hovels with clean, sunlit apartments.

Dr. Elliott, called by Mayor La Guardia the city's "Number One Good Neighbor," brought with him what, from today's vantage point, is an outmoded approach to community betterment. He was not an indigenous leader of his poor, unskilled neighbors, though he had lived among them for forty-seven years. He was college educated. He came from uptown. The money and political influence to support his efforts were

Down with an old slum, up with a new project.

supplied in the main by uptowners who believed in a middle-class, humanitarian approach to the problems of the poor. Later days were to see different and newer ways of neighborhood renewal, as the poor themselves demanded more and more of a say in the determination of their own destinies.

The Long Road Back

The John L. Elliott Houses were the first of the low-rent, city aided, public housing projects to be completed after the Second World War. So much time had elapsed since people had been "relocated" elsewhere to make way for the project, that many were scattered and never returned. Veterans—not necessarily from Chelsea—were given first choice. Thus only about half of the new apartments were filled with old residents of the neighborhood. Those who were fortunate enough to move out of filthy, over-crowded tenements into the spotless, airy apartments of the Elliott Houses found their new homes a haven and heaven. A few have never changed their minds.

Mrs. Beatrice Jennings, a resident of the Elliott Houses for the past twenty-six years, is one such person. She and her family were among those who were accepted from outside the neighborhood. Mrs. Jennings, presently a switchboard operator at the Hudson Guild, explains, "My husband and I and our two children lived in a small room with a single window on the West Side in upper Manhattan. We had to go one flight up to bathe and two flights down to wash or use the toilet. We had to eat sitting on the bed with a tray on our laps; there was just no room for a table and chairs." Mrs. Jennings continues,

My husband worked at night, and can you imagine what it was like to keep two small kids quiet in the day so he could get some sleep? And oh, my, when the weather was bad!

John L. Elliott Houses.

And then, one day, when the project first opened, I read an ad in the paper. The rental was something like twelve dollars a room per month. As I remember it, we were paying twenty dollars for our miserable hole-in-the-wall.

I said a little prayer and sent in the application. Two months later we were in!

Believe me, our new four-room apartment looked like a mansion. I think it was the sun coming in the windows as much as anything else. And imagine—a view of the river! Though we had to sleep on the floor in the beginning till we were able to buy beds, it was wonderful. And, it still seems that way, even though I'm now alone. I just wouldn't want to live anywhere else.

The Elliott Houses were built at minimum cost; the rooms are pitifully small, the walls are too thin to keep out sounds from other apartments, and such "frills" as doors on closets or covers on toilets were originally omitted.

This lack of amenities seems unimportant to Mrs. Jennings. The important thing is that Elliott Houses offered her and her black family the first decent housing that had ever been within their reach.

Originally, public housing was intended solely for those of limited income. As these people prospered, the theory was that they would then move out into other, better quarters. Unfortunately, in Chelsea as elsewhere, "other better quarters" were all too seldom available at moderate rentals.

Recently, the City Housing Authority has raised considerably the maximum income limits for tenants. This has been done not only because people who have pulled themselves up financially face the problem of having no place to go, but also because the Housing Authority believes that the goal of any housing project should be to include some economic as well as racial mixing, some stable, upwardly mobile families, as well as those on welfare.

During the last decade, Chelsea has been able to offer at

least a little additional housing to a number of families and single people in the lower income brackets. Two new public housing projects have now been added.

The housing was sorely needed, for even though some of the poor had moved out of the area newcomers were fast moving in. The most recent arrivals were the Puerto Ricans who, in search of a better life, started their migration to the mainland in the mid-forties.

The early 1960's saw the erection of Chelsea Houses, next door to the Elliott complex. These twenty-one story towers of tan-colored brick are separated by an open area that is pitifully small, drab, and littered.

Again we are invited to visit a family. Mrs. Earleam Sojourner, originally from South Carolina, and her eleven-year-old son, John Jr., greet us on our visit to their apartment. Reginald, aged seven, and four-year-old Malvin are still at school.

The rooms of the three bedroom apartment are a bit larger than those of the Elliott Houses. A dining area off the kitchen makes it possible to keep the living room free from mealtime furniture.

The Sojourners have been busy beautifying their apartment. The dining area is completely wood-panelled—a family project. Mr. Sojourner has cleverly used discarded die cuts to decorate the kitchen cabinets. The family has also installed an air conditioner to help make Chelsea summers more comfortable.

John Jr. likes his home, and enjoys meeting his friends in the open area outside. They play stoop ball and ring-a-lario, just as countless other city children have played for generations. "And then" says John, "Chelsea Park is only a block away. We play baseball and football there. But best of all, it's a place where I can ride my bike!"

We get a different picture from three teenage girls who live in the Elliott-Chelsea Houses; Vicky Van Leuvan, Linda Preston, and Alicia Hernandez.

Children of the city.

"We don't like living in Chelsea," they all agree at the start. "Too many purse snatchings, muggings, and drug addicts. The streets aren't safe and the hallways and elevators of our buildings are scary."

"I almost got kidnapped when I was smaller," Vicky declares.

"And there's really nothing for us to do after school. No place for girls to be safe outdoors," adds Linda.

"We come to the Hudson Guild because it keeps us off the streets—but there isn't much doing here for us," Alicia chimes in.

"But next week, they're starting something new—a special program for us teenagers—with clubs and parties and trips," one of the girls comments.

"How about school?" we ask, "Do you like it there?"

"Well," replies Vicky, "there's a neat new program in our junior high school this year. Our class is in the experiment and we really like it."

Vicky wants to be a tailor; Alicia hopes to go into nursing; Linda isn't sure yet. Special training in tailoring, nursing, and other skills is available in Chelsea's high schools.

"Perhaps Chelsea isn't such a bad place after all," one of the girls ventures to suggest with a grin.

The newest of Chelsea's public housing projects, opened in the late 60's, is federally aided Fulton Houses. The dreariness of the typical high-rise cluster has been overcome by combining eight, seven story buildings with three, twenty-five story structures. Since a quarter of the land is free of buildings, there are large, pleasant areas for recreation and outdoor sitting.

A portion of the project is devoted to the housing of large size families, families that have particular difficulty in finding adequate apartments. One of the most interesting features of Fulton Houses is the provision made for the elderly. On the ground floor is an attractive Community Center run by the

Hudson Guild for people over sixty. There are club rooms of all kinds, for classes, crafts, and games. There is a small gem of a garden, cared for by club members.

For its eight hundred patrons, most of whom live in the immediate neighborhood and in the housing development itself, the Community Center offers activity, companionship, and gaiety in place of the bleak loneliness of isolated old age.

In addition to the center, Fulton Houses has designed 74 of its 945 apartments especially for the aged. These apartments are provided with non-skid tile floors, stoves equipped with automatic shut-off devices, handles over bathtubs for grasping, and intercom systems for emergency help. Volunteer patrols escort aged tenants to their quarters at night.

We noted, in our visits to the three Chelsea projects built over the last quarter century, a marked improvement in design, the use of open space, and the services provided, in each succeeding development.

A significant number of Chelsea's aged are well taken care of. For some of the small children there is a fine nursery school and day care center run by the Hudson Guild. But the teenagers are the ones for whom no truly adequate provision has been made. A number of their parents are trying, through tenant organizations, to make things better for themselves, their children, and their neighbors.

The three projects; Elliott, Chelsea, and Fulton Houses cannot take care of the needs of many of the old-timers and newcomers among the area's low-income groups. But through the three developments, almost two thousand families and single people, half of them originally from Chelsea, have at the very least been supplied with living units many steps above the slum dwellings they previously occupied.

Public housing authorities in many cities—perhaps the one you live in—have come under heavy fire for their characterless, featureless, identical slabs of brick and mortar, sometimes

A Garden at Fulton Houses—planted and enjoyed by the elderly.

called "towers of frustration" and usually considered breeders of new slums.

People long in the field of Public Housing, as for example Catherine Bauer, the first research director of the United States Housing Authority, blame most of the trouble on the large-scale design of the projects. "Public housing skyscrapers," she states, "put occupants into a highly organized beehive of community life for which most American families have no desire and no aptitude. . . . There is no room in such schemes for individual deviation, for personal initiative and responsibility, for outdoor freedom and privacy. . . ."

Architectural critic, Jane Jacobs, opposes large scale slum clearance. She feels the disruption of neighborhood life caused by the replacement of low-rise slum buildings and institutions with public housing's high-rise superblocks, is responsible for the leaderlessness, isolation, and lack of safety in low-income projects.

Mrs. Marie McGuire, a former Federal Public Housing Administrator, states that "today 50 percent of the public housing tenants nationally are on welfare. . . . Families go to public housing at densities they've never had before and are expected to have responsibility for their neighbors and property . . . But where do we get the funds to provide the necessary services in order to give a family the full benefit of adjusting to a new environment?"

Where indeed, unless we, as citizens, see to it that adequate monies and talents are made available?

The belief that public housing can completely solve the problems of the poor has been proved untrue. Adequate housing is certainly important, but what quality of living such housing provides, what neighborliness it engenders, what other human needs it fulfills—these considerations are more important than the providing of mere shelter. Health, education, and job opportunities are all parts of the picture. We are at last recognizing these facts. Unfortunately, there are no easy solutions to these unsolved problems which exist in every city across our land.

The Co-op Story

New York City can point to other housing ventures in Chelsea, not only for people of low income, but for those of moderate income as well.

To understand the background of one of these developments, we must take a brief look at the northeast corner of Chelsea around Seventh Avenue and the Thirties—the heart of New York's Garment Center. It is this small area that supplies American women with 80 percent of their dresses, coats, and suits.

The industry itself has always been a murderously competitive commercial jungle, where it is said the "cloak and suiters, working on a one percent margin, drop like flies." In the early days of the industry, the garment workers, mostly Jewish immigrants in desperate need of employment, were mercilessly exploited. Years of injustice were followed by efforts at unionization, offering workers their only hope of improved conditions and a better life. A small, struggling union gradually developed into one of the strongest and most famous in the world—The International Ladies Garment Workers Union, or the ILGWU, as it is commonly called. In addition to improving wages and working conditions, the union has fostered many projects to enhance the lives of its members both at home and abroad. One such undertaking is a modern housing project in Chelsea.

In 1957, David Dubinsky, the dynamic President of the union, urged his General Executive Board to sponsor this development in conjunction with the United Housing Foundation, which is "a federation of non-profit organizations to promote better housing through cooperatives." The ILGWU Cooperative Houses (known also as Penn Station South), were designed primarily to help alleviate the acute shortage of decent housing for the union members and other middle-income wage earners. Furthermore, it was conceived as a walk-to-work community. Locating the project in midtown Manhattan would enable those residents engaged in the garment industry to live close to their jobs.

This was a novel idea, an idea that would make it possible and attractive for working people of moderate income to live close to their jobs in the central city. No more long hours of commuting in the crowded and stifling subways; hours would finally be freed for a fuller, richer life.

The best available site for the housing project, only a block from the Garment District, was one of the worst of Chelsea's deteriorated areas. It contained a mixture of loft and factory buildings, warehouses, parking lots, aging apartments, wholesale establishments, and a large number of three story row houses. These brownstones (as they were incorrectly called, for most of them were of brick) were remnants of Chelsea's better days. Many of the original one family dwellings had long since been converted into furnished rooming houses into whose miserable cubicles Irish, Jewish, Black, and Puerto Rican families were squeezed.

To start the new project and make efficient and economical use of the land, it was necessary to acquire the entire area at one time. Acquisition was made possible by organizing a company which, under state law, enabled the city to condemn the site.

The assessed value of the land and buildings was so high, however, that the carrying charges or upkeep of the new development might well have been too expensive for the wage earners for whom the project was being planned.

To solve this difficulty the sponsors of the project took advantage of the Federal Housing Act of 1949, whose stated purpose was "the realization as soon as feasible of the goal of a decent home and suitable living environment for every American family." "Private enterprise," the law further declared, "should be encouraged to serve as large a part of the total needs as possible." This urban renewal legislation was government's first attempt to attract private investment to the rebuilding of cities.

The land was purchased with the help of federal, state, and city funds. Construction costs were to be met by the 2,820 cooperating families, the union, and other private financial sources.

But before any building could take place, the entire site was to be cleared. This meant, first and foremost, the relocation of families and businesses into dwellings and quarters that met the standards set by the city and the Federal Government. Rehousing 2,600 site families "with decent, safe and sanitary housing within their means" was a difficult, almost impossible task, and often a heartbreaking one. However, in little more than a year, relocation was complete and the development under way. In May of 1962, families started moving in. Though it was "first come, first served," priorities were given to occupants who had lived on the site at the time the property was acquired. As so often happens, there were many who could not afford to move back. The purchasing price of $650 per room was astronomical to most former residents. Nevertheless, when the co-op was finally complete, three hundred original site families had bought apartments in the development.

ILGWU members were naturally among the first to move in. They had signed up for and paid deposits on apartments selected from blueprints, five years before their new homes became a reality.

Mrs. Bella Hyman is one of these union members. She and her husband, who is no longer living, selected a corner apartment on the ninth floor of one of the units. "We trusted the blueprint," Mrs. Hyman tells us, "and we took pot luck." She has a charming apartment, with well proportioned rooms, wide windows, and a prized balcony. "I just *live* out here, meals and all, during the warm months," Mrs. Hyman declares.

We ask her to tell us more about the cooperative that owns and operates the project. "We are it," she replies. "We who live here are all member-stockholders, running our own community through an elected Board of Directors. They select a professional manager. Then there are what seem like hundreds of committees to help along. Our membership is open to *all*, regardless of race or religion. We're really a United Nations in miniature," she says with a smile.

"Are there any limitations on the income of the cooperators?" we ask.

"Yes, our income may not be more than eight times the yearly carrying charges, or what you might call rent."

"And aside from an attractive apartment is life good here?"

"Is it!" Mrs. Hyman exclaims. "There's something doing all the time. We've a beautiful community room for parties and meetings. There are recreation rooms for the youngsters. I personally belong to half a dozen groups like the Workman's Circle, the Golden Ring, the Pioneer Women. We've a theater and movie house without having to travel at night for our entertainment. And we can enjoy the outdoors right here—not ten blocks away.

Mrs. Hyman paused for breath, then added triumphantly, "Five hundred families on the waiting list; we're the lucky ones. See how wonderful we live!"

Our hostess takes us on tour around and through the development. It is a veritable city within a city, including living quarters for almost three thousand families, its own heating

The site of the co-op—before.

The site of the co-op—after.

and cooling plant, a co-op supermarket, a theater, recreational facilities, and a number of small stores and offices. The project in its overwhelming entirety has nevertheless an inviting atmosphere. This is due in part to the hundreds of balconies that dot its red brick facade. These small outdoor areas allow people living in skyscrapers in the central city to enjoy a bit of the out-of-doors right on their own porches, high above the noise and bustle.

Best of all, 65 percent of the entire area in the development is free of buildings, so that there is ample room for gardens and grassy plots, for play space and sitting areas, for walks shaded by trees and made colorful by flowering shrubs. One plot of land has been turned into a public playground for the benefit of the larger Chelsea community.

We are particularly impressed with the upkeep of each foyer and corridor of the buildings through which we pass. The tiled walls look as though they have been freshly scrubbed. The floors are clean and unlittered. One can see at a glance that thought, care, and hard work have gone into the maintenance of the commonly shared parts of the co-op.

The House Committee has been busy, too, in organizing a volunteer patrol during evening hours. "Yes," explains Mrs. Hyman, "we ourselves help the police protect our homes from intruders. We simply sit in the lobbies and check on the people who enter. Our neighborhood isn't free of crime. There are,sad to say, purse snatchings, muggings and robberies. But the police tell us that Chelsea has one of the lowest crime rates in the city."

This is a change from the Chelsea of the early 1900's! Then it was said that John Elliott was the only man who could safely walk the neighborhood's streets at night, with a gold watch chain showing.

Penn Station South or ILGWU Houses is a far cry from the slums it displaced. The walk-to-work-and-play co-op offers some six thousand people of modest income new homes and a new life.

Is there something about cooperative ownership that gives people a special sense of pride—pride not only in their own living units but also in their commonly shared facilities? Is the co-op idea the key to better living even in a high-rise situation? Or are other factors, such as the possession of skills, jobs, and good health still more important influences?

Government officials and others are beginning to wonder whether they have made a mistake in subsidizing housing rather than people. Today experiments are being conducted that supply direct supplements or subsidies to the needy so that they may move into cooperatives or private housing. Will these experiments prove successful?

Even if they are successful, will subsidies to a scattering of individuals or families ever be sufficient in quantity to do away with the need for massive new public housing developments of some description?

There are no ready answers to these questions. Trial and error, flexibility and willingness to learn from mistakes should help those concerned and responsible, to make new and creative choices.

The Brownstones

Some of Chelsea's old timers living in dilapidated quarters were able through the years to improve their financial lot. Instead of moving away, they decided to stay in the area that was home to them. And so, they bought old single family houses that were still sound enough for occupancy.

These old-time residents have now been joined by new-comers, many of them young couples with small families; artists, writers, actors, and young business executives among them. These are the people who took a look at Chelsea and liked it for its convenient location, its cosmopolitan nature, and its new air of liveliness and rejuvenation.

At first the single family houses, or brownstones, were to be had for a few thousand dollars; later, as the demand grew, the prices rose. Most desirable were the Greek Revival houses that face the General Theological Seminary with its tree-shaded lawns surrounding old, ivy-covered buildings. This area, Chelsea Square, once part of Clement Moore's farm, is one of the only park-like spots left in the neighborhood.

To learn more of the brownstone story first hand, we decide to visit two homes not far from Chelsea Square. The old town houses in this area are sandwiched between two industrial sections. To the east are small clothing, furniture, and printing establishments. To the west is a larger manufacturing and warehousing district. Some of the lofts, briefly converted in the early 1900's to motion picture studios, are today used mainly for food storage and printing plants.

Our first visit is to Lewis and Harriet Winter who live in their new-old home with their three children; two grown daughters and a pre-school son.

"We wanted to live in the city," declares Mr. Winter, "to escape a middle-class ghetto on Long Island. Suburbia had all the wrong things for us—country club, crabgrass, and cars. When I look back, it was really 'nowheres.' Here our kids are thrown into life and it's for real!"

"I guess," adds Mrs. Winter, "children grow up best where their parents are happy."

When the Winters decided to become city dwellers they were attracted to Chelsea because the low town houses on Twentieth Street provided both sunlight and open sky. The house they bought in the mid 1960's was a shambles, and for that reason was priced within their means. The Winters' brownstone had deteriorated into a typical rooming house; fourteen

The green heart of Chelsea, the General Theological Seminary.

tiny rooms in all, with five people to a room. Such crowding finally became illegal, and it was no longer profitable for the owner to hold and maintain his property, so he decided to sell it. The Winters ripped out partitions and made the house over as a comfortable, colorful home with an atmosphere of warmth and welcome.

"When we started digging in the backyard," Harriet Winter relates, "we found some kind of an ancient pathway; and also a stone-lined basin in which we think some long forgotten housewife may have washed her family's clothes."

The Winters have made the backyard a flowering garden, shaded by a white dogwood tree. They have transported the woods to West Twentieth Street with jack-in-the-pulpit and ferns, wild strawberries, and columbine. This family may have "escaped" to the city but they have brought with them the much-loved delights of the countryside.

Susan and Bill Shanok are our second hosts. Bill works in Brooklyn, where he is vice president of a large plastics company. "Only twenty minutes by car," says Bill, "and that makes commuting a pleasure."

"That's only one of the reasons we chose Chelsea," adds Susan, who is a writer. "There are lots of others. We liked the small town feeling, the block parties, the general air of neighborliness. We think it's a good place for our baby daughter to grow up."

The young couple was first attracted to the house, built on Clarke's property in 1835, by the beauty of its eyebrow-arch doorway, fashioned of hand-chiselled brownstone surrounded by a roped scroll, hand-carved in wood. People called it "the most beautiful door in the city."

The Shanoks bought their home in 1967 for what must have been a good stiff price. They then proceeded to rip down walls and build an extension in the back, creating large new rooms and balconies.

They have brought fascinating imports from all over the

world into their new home—parquet flooring from Thailand, kitchen tiles from Mexico, Early American antiques from Mrs. Shanok's New England forebears.

The Shanoks are active leaders in their block association, which, while attempting to break down the walls that separate neighbors from each other, is also trying to spruce up the block itself.

We learn more about the Chelsea block associations, similar to such associations in many other cities, through several telephone conversations.

Mrs. Jacqueline Schwartzman, a native of Chelsea and today a brownstoner, is the founder of one such organization. Smoking chimneys, filthy streets, decayed buildings—these were some of the issues that first drew the homeowners and tenants of West Twenty-second Street together.

Sparked by Mrs. Schwartzman, in 1966 the group formally organized itself into a block association. Their first job was to educate themselves on existing laws on smokestack emissions, garbage disposal, permissible size of trucks on a residential street, and noise control. Doggedly they contacted the appropriate public agencies and the police. Next, they concentrated on the beautification and health of their block; clean-ups, tree plantings, and "starve-a-rat" campaigns were among their efforts.

Now, when special issues concerning the general welfare of Chelsea come up, the Twenty-second Street Block Association is equipped to organize support or protest, as the case may be.

We also learn about the Twenty-fourth Street Block Association. This group has a yearly flower sale at which garden plants for back yards, window box plants, potting soil, and other gardening accessories are sold at extremely reasonable prices. The sale takes place in the dreary front yard of a rooming house, which once a year, is magically transformed into a colorful flowering garden. Neighbors who have never before spoken to each other exchange greetings and smiles.

Some of the money raised by the sale is used to send neighborhood youngsters to summer camp.

From our contacts with the brownstoners we observe that they are eager to share in the life of their new community. From the Winters and Shanoks we also learn that each of the families believes firmly in public education. But the Winters, with a child almost ready for school, feel that today's problems in the public schools are so overwhelming that they might reluctantly have to seek a private school for their son. Mrs. Shanok, who has a toddler daughter, is already meeting with other neighborhood parents in an attempt to strengthen the public schools; this in anticipation of the day when their young ones will be ready to attend.

In speaking of their blocks, both families say that they like the racial mix but balk at the frightening doings of a few of their neighbors. "An ethnic mix, yes" they seem to be saying, "and an economic mix, too. But if only it could be a mix with compatible standards of living and behavior."

This is an understandable feeling. The trouble is that the people with the "incompatible" ways are often those at the bottom of the economic scale, the most recent arrivals, the ones as yet unfamiliar with the customs of a strange, new world.

Increasing demands on Chelsea sites—for salvageable town houses, for new luxury apartments—are helping to push the poorest residents out of the area. When "upgrading" is finally accomplished, there is a danger that the former slums will be exchanged for what the Winters came to Chelsea to avoid—another middle-class ghetto.

Today's Waterfront

Another perplexing Chelsea problem, but one that may be easier to solve than the "people" problem, is that of the area's decaying and dying waterfront.

Fire escape—escape from a tenement.

The difficulty is this: just as sailboats were left behind by the advent of steam, so steamboats, both passenger and cargo, have to a great extent lost out to air transport. The great American trans-Atlantic liners have finally called it a day, and the cargo vessels now in operation have found a better port than Chelsea.

Cargo shipping has, in the last decade or so, undergone a major revolution. Less and less do longshoremen heave or fork-lift countless individual bundles of assorted sizes. Today, more and more cargo is placed in gigantic metal containers and packed and sealed in distant factories. Once at the dock, these receptacles are mechanically loaded into large container ships looking more like floating crates than seagoing vessels.

The new container ships have not been docking at Chelsea's piers. Instead, they make for the efficient modern facilities, built by the Port of New York Authority and located at Port Elizabeth on the New Jersey side of the Hudson. These facilities, unlike the ones on the Manhattan side, have ample space for the loading and unloading of the containers onto trucks.

And so Chelsea's docks and piers—some fairly new ones at that—had to close shop in 1968. Once deserted, they began to deteriorate rapidly. The days when longshoremen scurried to be head of the line, waiting for the daily "shape up," or hiring session, seemed over. The burly men who gave the area so much of its tough and salty flavor kept lining up, but not for work. They were lining up to receive the stipend guaranteed them by their union contract.

In the summer of '72, an announcement came from the Mayor's office that four inactive piers on the Chelsea waterfront were to be reopened as an air cargo distribution center for the metropolitan area. The purpose was to relieve pressure at Kennedy International Airport. To solve the problem of traffic congestion, the movement of the cargo from the airport to the pier center was planned for the slack traffic hours, between midnight and six in the morning.

The piers of Chelsea, a dying resource.

According to the Mayor, the reopening of the piers will eventually mean 500 dock and transportation jobs, and 1,500 more in related industries. Should this operation prove successful, it will be a major step in reviving Chelsea's waterfront, welcomed not only by the longshoremen but by residents in general.

Several other schemes for the waterfront have however been vigorously fought off by the neighborhood. The Federal Aviation Agency, for example, wanted to construct a floating STOL port for short-take-off-and-landing planes in the waters directly off Chelsea. The people of the neighborhood, aware of the noise, traffic congestion, and danger the STOL port would bring, were violently and vocally opposed to the idea, and they voiced their opposition through their local groups. The plan was dropped even before the FAA had made an application to the Department of City Planning.

The department itself has issued suggestions for the rehabilitation of the city's waterfront. Among the ideas for Chelsea is a dual use industrial-residential mix that would allow the roofing of the elevated West Side Highway and the building of 6,500 low and middle-income apartments on the deck thus provided.

The community's desires and goals are supported and strengthened by their various neighborhood groups including the municipally supported Chelsea Neighborhood Conservation Program and the numerous block associations. In addition, there is a local district planning board. Other cities have similar groups, associations, and boards. How responsive or representative all of these groups are, particularly to the needs of the least articulate and the poorest, is still an open question.

Another voice expressing community concern through its news coverage and editorial comment, is the local weekly, the *Chelsea Clinton News*. Bruce Buckley, the young editor of the paper, comments:

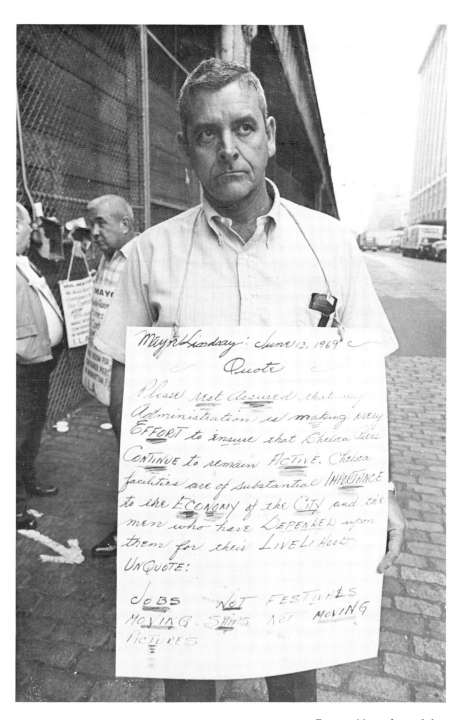

The sign reads:

Mayor Lindsay: June 13, 1969
Quote

Please rest assured that my
Administration is making every
EFFORT to ensure that Chelsea Piers
CONTINUE to remain ACTIVE. Chelsea
facilities are of substantial IMPORTANCE
to the ECONOMY of the CITY and the
men who have DEPENDED upon
them for their LIVELIHOOD.
UNQUOTE!

JOBS   NOT FESTIVALS
MOVING SHIPS NOT MOVING
PICTURES

Fewer ships—fewer jobs.

A number of the people in Chelsea have a pretty good idea of the way they'd like to see the waterfront developed—renovation of buildings suited for renewal, new desperately needed low and middle-income housing where ancient structures should be torn down. And more jobs for our longshoremen should be at the very top of our priority list.

Then there ought to be certain areas devoted to playgrounds and parks. Why, there's hardly a spot of open space in Chelsea where people can breathe free. And think what it would mean to create some honest-to-goodness greenery right at our own waterfront!

He pauses. "All this—a waterfront with jobs, housing and open spaces—and other things, too, might just happen," he concludes, "because there are a lot of people in Chelsea who have always cared and still care."

The Cost of Change

Chelsea's worst slums have given way to improved buildings—the massive co-op, public housing complexes, renovated brownstones. The benefits are plain to see as you walk the streets of Chelsea today.

The costs are not so visible. They are tucked away in individual human lives. The upgrading of the neighborhood has spelled dispossession for certain of Chelsea's residents—usually its poorest. Where did these people go after they were forced to leave their miserable shelters?

Let us take, as an example, the most recent outcasts, those ousted from rooming houses bought for restoration. Social workers and housing authorities tell us that the displaced tenants were relocated: some of the old men to a seamen's home, others from among the elderly and a few of the families to public housing in the neighborhood, all the rest to other neighborhoods. Many of these people had a deep attachment to a particular spot, even if it was only a single dingy room on a familiar block. It was inevitable that they would be uprooted and transplanted. There seemed to be no other choice, for there was not enough decent housing to go around. There still is not.

Actually, there may be a new choice—a more flexible way of upgrading neighborhoods without so much heartbreaking disruption of people's lives.

Instead of bulldozing huge tracts for massive redevelopment projects, so costly in time and in displaced lives, why not build vest pocket housing on small vacant lots? Then people can move in before they are forced out of purchased townhouses or before old, unsalvageable tenements are torn down. This plan is being tried in Coney Island as we shall learn in detail in the next part of this book.

But the experiment has not been tried in Chelsea. And so you will find dispossessed Chelsea people in many other sections of the city. You will find them in crowded slums where their problems and the problems of their new neighborhoods are fast multiplying.

One social worker feels that eventually the poor will all be pushed out of areas like Chelsea into the Bronx—just above Manhattan—where there is still a bit of available housing. "And then," she declares, "we will have created in the new ghetto a jungle, the likes of which we've never even imagined."

Nancy Linday, whom we meet on one of our last visits, tells us what it was like to be shoved out of Chelsea and into the Bronx.

Nancy, just out of her teens, relates that her family had been one of those relocated when the ILGWU co-op went up. "I was eleven years old at the time, and my father had lived in Chelsea for thirty-five years—just about all his life."

"We were bitter," she continues. "We had been living in a

four-room apartment at forty-five dollars a month, and how could we possibly buy a home in the co-op at six hundred and fifty dollars a room? We couldn't! So we were finally relocated in the Bronx. We were just miserable. Somehow, we couldn't take hold there. I guess, when they tore us up from Chelsea, they left our roots behind." She smiles. "And here I am back again, spending my spare time where my roots are. Some day I want to live here, if I can find an apartment to fit my pocketbook. Today that's impossible—at least in a place I'd want to live in."

Nancy explains that in college she made a study of urban open space and that she took as her project the drafting of a proposal for the renovation of the Chelsea-Elliott play areas, the very areas that had seemed so hopelessly drab and dismal to us.

One of Nancy's ideas is to create play spaces in which children can discover their own physical resources through exploration and creative play. She feels the problem is not one of space, but rather of design.

Not waiting for her carefully thought-out proposals to gain total acceptance, Nancy set out to work on a small segment of the transformation. Armed with $500 from the Twenty-fourth Street Block Association, supplied with lumber from a demolished building, and guided by professional designs, Nancy was ready to begin.

With the help of three teenagers from the Neighborhood Youth Corps, a Treehouse Climber soon rose in a once gloomy spot between the tall buildings of the housing complex.

Nancy takes us over to see the fanciful but sturdy structure. Children of assorted ages are busily playing and climbing. "Next week a bunch of kids will be painting it. And then . . ." she pauses. "Then it will be on to the next!"

Nancy is training to be a social worker, and our guess is that

Building a Treehouse Climber for creative play.

having rediscovered her roots in Chelsea, this is where she will eventually decide to live and work, and help her neighbors thrive.

But thriving in Chelsea is still fraught with dangers and threats, especially for the poor who remain there.

There is the ever-present threat implicit in the scarce supply of land—land not only needed for housing, but for other uses as well. The United States Post Office, for example, had chosen a Chelsea site for expanded operations. The people of Chelsea protested, for it meant the loss of an enclosed swimming pool and recreation area. Restoration of these community resources on another spot was promised. The enlarged Post Office is there; up to this time the swimming pool is not.

Then, too, as property in this conveniently located part of the city continues to increase in value, developers will find that office buildings are an even better financial investment than luxury housing. How will this economic consideration affect the future of Chelsea? Will the people who live in the neighborhood and love it be able to speak with one voice and exercise enough political power to stem the tide of economic "progress" in the future?

The rebirth and saving of Chelsea have been accomplished up to this point because there have been people who cared and who translated their caring into constructive action.

One person in particular who cared deeply and acted courageously was Dorothy Kenyon, former Civil Court Judge of the district, whom we visited shortly before her death. Judge Kenyon, a tall, greyhaired woman, young in spirit though getting on in years, was involved in the fight for a better Chelsea. To further this end, she remained an active member of various local committees and councils to the end of her life.

"I love Chelsea" she declared. "Yes, I've lived here for over forty years." The "here" is a twelve story apartment house opposite the Seminary on Twenty-first Street. Consumers Co-

A Chelsea champion—Judge Dorothy Kenyon.

operative Services built the sixty-seven unit residence in 1930. The cooperators were mostly young couples of meager or moderate means.

"We tore down five lovely brownstones to build this house, but somehow, with its soft red brick, and casement windows eleven feet wide in all our living rooms, our vest pocket yard in front, and our small, shared garden in the back, it looks very cosy and completely at home among the older brownstones."

Judge Kenyon went on, "The small brook that ran through Clarke's old apple orchard still flows through the sub-sub-cellar of our house. Sometimes I think I hear it at night," she smiled, "at least in my dreams."

Judge Kenyon knew John Elliott well. She remembered him, fearlessly roaming the dark streets late in the evening, puffing his ever-present pipe, while pledging his faith to his poor neighbors and to the little lost children he discovered sleeping in doorways. "He led the Chelsea of his day to a better life by insisting it was a job they must all do together; and they did."

"But," declared Judge Kenyon, "the problem isn't solved by any means. The poor of Chelsea are still confronted with the hopelessness of poverty, the cruelty of bias, the growing alienation of each from the other, the threat of eviction from the only homes they have ever known."

"Community change," she continued, "always involves suffering, but must the worst suffering fall almost wholly on the poor? Isn't there a chance of finding a middle way by those of us who have some voice and possibly some choice in the matter?"

Judge Kenyon concluded emphatically, "Can't we choose to preserve *all* of Chelsea—integrated as we truly are now, with our great variety of national origins, our economic and cultural differences?" The people of Chelsea, Dorothy Kenyon believed, can make this choice by concerted action, if they have the will to do so.

Half a century ago, John Elliott wrote, "We need a faith that the human desert that covers such great areas in every city has the power of self-transformation." Today, so many years after Dr. Elliott's time, the transformation of Chelsea's desert is slowly taking shape, though serious obstacles and recognized dangers remain to be overcome.

So let us take leave of Chelsea as its people continue their long, hard struggle to make the desert bloom. We will look at another of the city's blighted areas—an area with a shorter and more recent cycle of growth, decay, and rebuilding.

In Chelsea, John Elliott, the ILGWU, and the brownstoners did what they felt was best, and the residents of the community accepted their actions without a murmur. This was in the 1900-1950 era. The story is different today. Let us watch it unfold as we turn to our next neighborhood.

PART TWO

CONEY ISLAND

Community of Many Voices

Fun Capitol

Walk a dozen blocks away from Chelsea and ask a passerby on the street to direct you there. Chances are you will draw a blank stare. "Chelsea? What's that?"

Few city neighborhoods are familiar to the people outside their narrow boundaries. Have you heard of Russian Hill? It is in San Francisco. And how many Chicago residents can lead a stranger to Back-of-the-Yards . . . which is in their backyard?

There is, however, one city neighborhood which has been famous even beyond its country's borders for a century or more. Most New Yorkers, and especially young ones, can tell us where to find it.

Coney Island! What picture does the name conjure up for you? Is it the headlines in newspapers on hot summer days: "ONE MILLION PEOPLE SEEK RELIEF FROM HEAT" on Coney Island's public beaches? Or is it the taste of the Coney Island hot dog, dripping with sauerkraut and spiced with mustard?

For generations of children and their parents, the image of Coney Island has been "Fun"—great, glittering amusement parks called Steeplechase, Luna Park, and Dreamland, or the spectacular fireworks displays which have been set off over the

A hot day in the city means a crowded beach at Coney Island.

ocean once a week, for a hundred years. "Coney Island taught a puritan nation how to play" was the description of its role in the nineteenth century.

Coney Island is a narrow five mile strip of sand which juts out into New York Harbor from the tip of the Borough of Brooklyn. The Indians treasured it for the hard shell clams which they found there so abundantly, and which they used as money. After them, the farmers of nearby Gravesend used the little island as a winter grazing area for their cattle; sedge grass grew behind the sand dunes. The creek which separated the island from the mainland was shallow at low tide, and could be waded across.

Out of the shells which were so plentiful, a road was built across Coney Island Creek in 1829, by a group calling itself the Coney Island Road and Bridge Company. They hoped to make money by charging a toll for carriages which were driven across to the beautiful beach.

Soon as many as three hundred carriages a day were crossing the creek. Well-to-do Brooklyn families enjoyed the drive along the shore, the bright sunshine, and the sea-breeze. A hotel and restaurant, the Coney Island House, was built by the Road and Bridge Company, and the fashionable and famous flocked to this pleasant, novel playground, a seaside resort. One of them was Walt Whitman, the poet, and he wrote that he loved "to race up and down the hard sand, and declaim Homer or Shakespeare to the surf and the seagulls by the hour."

Throughout the nineteenth and early twentieth centuries, the summer resort expanded. Transportation was the key to its growth. In addition to the carriages, there were soon steamboats bringing pleasure seekers to the seashore from Brooklyn and Manhattan. Then, as the railroads extended out to Coney Island, the number of visitors on a summer day climbed into the tens of thousands.

More vast hotels were built along the beaches to accommodate the crowds who wanted to vacation at the shore. To amuse them and the many customers who came to Coney for a day's outing, new forms of entertainment were constantly developed by enterprising showmen.

Bathing in the sea was first introduced in America at Coney Island, in the 1800's. At first only the brave tried it and there was a great debate over how one should dress for this adventure. Overton's Coney Island Directory for 1883 rules: "The dress should consist of two parts—a pair of pantaloons and a blouse; the latter should not fit too tightly."

Thousands of bathhouses were built along the beach where swimmers could change their clothes for a fee. For those who did not wish to pay the price, however, there were other choices. Norman Rosten, the author of *Under the Boardwalk,* grew up in a house in Coney Island which had lockers and showers for bathers, in the basement. As a boy it was his job to prowl the streets of Coney Island for customers, shouting "Lockers with showers, twenty-five cents!" Cheapest of all were those who put their bathing suits on under their clothes, before leaving for the beach. Local merchants referred to them, scornfully, as the "drippers."

For thirty years, until 1910, Coney Island was the horse racing capital of the East. There were three tracks there and in neighboring Gravesend and the sporting crowd, rich and poor, made Coney its summer headquarters. The newspaper, the *Brooklyn Eagle,* described the scene in the 1880's: "After the races the losers took the first train back to the City and the winners rushed to the Manhattan Beach Hotel for a cooling plunge, a two inch porterhouse, and washed it down with burgundy and champagne."

With the rich and the racing crowd vying for rooms at Coney Island's hotels, their corridors were sometimes set up with cots for the overflow guests on weekends. On a Friday

The new sport in 1866 is sea bathing at Coney Island.

MOVING BRIGHTON BEACH HOTEL, CONEY ISLAND, WITH LOCOMOTIVES.

The sea advances—the hotel recedes. Brighton Beach, 1888.

night during the racing season the trains going out to the beach were sometimes seventeen cars long.

For a day or for a summer, by boat and rail and carriage, from all parts of the East Coast, people flocked to Coney Island to enjoy themselves. The sea air stimulated their appetites and restaurants and saloons flourished. A favorite food was Coney Island clams. Diners relished raw clams on the half shell and Coney Island clam chowder.

In fact, in the early 1900's, the biggest restaurant in the world was in Coney Island. It was run by a German immigrant, Charles Feltman, the man who first put a hot sausage inside a roll thus inventing that staple of the American diet, the hot dog.

Gaily painted carrousels were imported from Europe and introduced at Coney Island. George Tilyou, an entertainment entrepreneur, brought the Ferris Wheel there in 1893. There were roller coasters, the Tunnel of Love, sideshows with freaks, and games of skill and chance. Tilyou gathered dozens of these attractions together and opened an amusement park, called Steeplechase, in 1897.

The amusement park was so successful that it was soon imitated. The next to appear was Luna Park, in 1903, and then two years later, Dreamland opened. The buildings at Dreamland were elaborately decorated with spires, minarets, and towers which were brilliantly outlined, at night, by hundreds of thousands of the new electric light bulbs. For those aboard a ship sailing to New York at night, the lights of Luna Park and Dreamland were the first thing they saw as they entered the harbor.

The Russian writer, Maxim Gorki, described this vision: "With the advent of night a fantastic city all of fire suddenly rises from the ocean into the sky. Thousands of ruddy sparks glimmer in the darkness, limning in fine, sensitive outline on the black background of the sky shapely towers of miraculous castles, palaces and temples. Golden gossamer threads trem-

Amusement park at night—city of fire.

ble in the air. They intertwine in transparent flaming patterns, which flutter and melt away, in love with their own beauty mirrored in the waves. Fabulous beyond conceiving, ineffably beautiful, is this fiery scintillation."

Inside the amusement parks the thrills were earthier. Tilyou, the amusement park pioneer, said Steeplechase's success was based on his theory that "most people never grow up." He gave his customers thirty-one rides to choose from, for fifty cents. There was a Whichaway which whirled you in four directions, in rapid and dizzying succession. And the Barrel of Love whirled you round and round down a sharp incline.

Most popular of all at Steeplechase was the Blowhole Theatre. Unsuspecting customers were led across a stage, when suddenly a clown prodded the men with a stick which gave them a slight electrical shock. Ladies were tenderly guided over holes in the floor with air jets hidden below, which abruptly blew their skirts up over their heads. The embarrassment and surprise of the victims on stage provided endless entertainment for the audience hidden in the darkened auditorium.

The pattern of amusement at Coney Island was copied all over the world, from Buenos Aires to Berlin. And new seaside resorts were built along the Atlantic Coast, catering to the taste for summering at the beach which Coney had first exploited. They beckoned to the rich and fashionable who had made Coney Island their summer headquarters for thirty years.

During those boom years, Coney Island had been governed by the independent town of Gravesend. The Supervisors of the town encouraged any money-making proposition, including gambling, horse racing, and prize fighting which were banned elsewhere in New York City. The religious leaders, and respectable citizens of neighboring Brooklyn were scandalized and called the wicked place "Sodom by the Sea." They were particularly opposed to the horse racing and gambling at Coney's

Strolling on Surf Avenue, 1896.

tracks. For years they petitioned the State Legislature to crack down on the impious town and put Gravesend and Coney Island under Brooklyn's rule. In 1910, a reform minded State Legislature took that step. The race tracks were shut down, the gambling ended.

To Coney by Subway

The rich and the fashionable who had filled the big summer homes at Seagate, at the western end of Coney Island, and patronized the elaborate beach hotels in Brighton Beach and Manhattan Beach, at the eastern half, drifted away to newer playgrounds. Some hotels went bankrupt and were razed; others burned down. In their place cheaper summer rental housing was built to fit the budget of vacationers of modest means. An example of this is the half dozen bungalows built in 1916, on a Coney Island side street, for $550 each.

The subway came to Coney Island in 1920, and so more and more families came out to the beach just for the day. It cost five cents to escape from the hot streets of the city to Coney and the customers came by the millions. This was the era of the "nickel empire." Feltman's elegant dining pavilions were too expensive for these customers. The subway clientele flocked to an open air stand on Surf Avenue founded, in 1916, by one of Feltman's waiters. Huge signs proclaimed it as "NATHAN'S FAMOUS 5¢ HOT DOGS." It is still there, but when we checked it last the price had risen to forty cents (with all the ketchup, mustard and sauerkraut you could eat).

One by one the spacious amusement parks closed down. The last to close was Steeplechase, in 1965. In their place individual rides, games of chance, and shooting galleries fill the side streets and Surf Avenue. Instead of entertainment from one end of the island to the other, customers find their fun only

Coney's favorite food—Nathan's famous frankfurters.

in an eighteen block area in part of the section of Coney called West Brighton.

Let us go and see Coney Island as it is now. How shall we get there from Chelsea? Coney is accessible by boat and car, but the greatest number of people come by subway, which there becomes an elevated track above the street.

The ride out from Manhattan will take nearly an hour. At first we will travel under the crowded streets of midtown Manhattan, and through a tunnel under the East River to downtown Brooklyn. Past Brooklyn's business district the train will emerge and take us on elevated tracks above the less densely developed parts of the borough.

When we are within sight of the end of Brooklyn we see it reaching out into the harbor. The train is rattling along now through a city landscape of low apartment houses, small factories, and streets of closely packed one and two family houses. Ahead of us, suddenly, looms a wall of brick; a row of towering apartment houses over twenty stories high. This is our first glimpse of Coney Island's new skyline—hardly as picturesque as the glittering one which greeted Maxim Gorki as he sailed toward it.

Our subway train crosses Shell Road, covered now with asphalt and the rusty, old elevated structure. It still retains the name and perhaps, deep down below, a few of the old clam shells remain. There are four sections of Coney Island, and subway trains travel through only two of them before reaching the last terminal, Stillwell Avenue, in the heart of the entertainment area. If we were to take some binoculars and ride up in the elevator to one of the terraces jutting out of those tall apartment houses we sighted we could get a clearer idea of the whole Coney Island community. Let us get our bearings before we zero in on the life of the people of this neighborhood—a neighborhood in transition.

Looking toward the eastern end of the island, where the

land reaches out into Sheepshead Bay, Coney forms a narrow peninsula, a mile long, surrounded by the bay and the Atlantic Ocean. At the tip are the buildings of Kingsborough Community College, which is a part of the City University.

The other buildings in the area are residential, one and two story private homes, set well apart from each other. Along the Atlantic there is a large public beachfront park, with grassy playing fields and picnic grounds. No stores, apartment houses, or elevated tracks intrude into this expensive, residential corner of Coney Island.

Manhattan Beach, its residents tell us, is a great place to live, winter or summer. Swimming, the views of ocean and bay, and the abundant opportunities for those who like fishing and boating have made it desirable, as a summer resort in the nineteenth century, and as a year-round residence now. Houses in this pleasant area range in price from $25,000 to $100,000.

The section which adjoins it, on the west, is Brighton Beach. It is two miles long and several blocks wider than Manhattan Beach. Elevated tracks run through it, above the main shopping street, Brighton Beach Avenue. In the shadow of the tracks there are many small stores and restaurants which serve the people who live nearby, in the houses and apartment buildings which fill the side streets.

Walking along Brighton Beach Avenue, peering into pizza parlors, chop suey shops, or delicatessens fragrant with the spicy smell of hot pastrami, we note that many of the customers are elderly. Brighton Beach has the highest concentration of people over fifty years old in New York City; half of its population is in that age bracket.

Along the ocean there is a wide, sandy beach and a wooden boardwalk which runs alongside it. The boardwalk, and the subway, continue westward, across a broad avenue called Ocean Parkway. This forms the boundary line between Brighton Beach and West Brighton. The subway ends halfway through West Brighton, at Stillwell Avenue.

West Brighton is the most complex, varied, and rapidly changing part of Coney Island. It contains half of the land of Coney Island and the majority of its 40,000 people. It has more than its share of the problems. At the Ocean Parkway end of West Brighton are soaring, modern apartment houses. From the balconies of their apartments those who live here can gaze out at the wide watery horizon, or the roller coasters and ferris wheel just outside their residential area. A public beach and boardwalk lined with food stands and exaggerated billboards, run for two and a half miles through West Brighton.

Winter or summer, many elderly people sit on the benches which face the ocean and sun themselves. Year-round, children dig in the sand, building castles, tunnels, and moats which the ocean fills.

Beyond the honky-tonk of the Stillwell Avenue entertainment area, West Brighton continues westward into a section of shabby residential buildings. The side streets are lined with aged two and three story houses of wood and brick. Some are boarded up, and others have been torn down and replaced by vacant lots filled with rubble and garbage.

Along the avenues, and elsewhere, in sharp contrast to this decay, are groups of sturdy brick apartment buildings. Interspersed between the dilapidated houses and the modern apartments are clusters of half finished buildings, surrounded by machinery. Placards at these sites repeatedly proclaim that this new housing is being built under programs financed by the City, State, or Federal Government.

Continuing westward across Coney Island we arrive at Seagate, separated forbiddingly from West Brighton by a twelve foot high wire fence. Beyond the fence lies a half mile triangle of land surrounded by the waters of Gravesend Bay. Within the borders of Seagate some seven hundred families are comfortably and safely housed. There are only one and two family houses, some set off by spacious lawns, others crowded close together. The streets are pleasantly shaded by trees and neither apartment houses nor stores intrude. If we wanted to visit Seagate we would have to pass through a gate manned by private guards. And we would only be allowed to enter if we were the guests of a resident of Seagate.

Housing-Response to Pressure

Coney Island is a neighborhood which is geographically one, but whose sections have developed, during the past 150 years, in different ways. The sections affect each other, even when they try to fence each other out. And all of Coney Island has changed, and is still changing, in response to the pressures of New York City.

We have seen some of these pressures, and the responses to them, in Chelsea. The shortage of good, middle-income housing which inspired the renewal of the brownstones in Chelsea is parallelled by the conversion of summer homes into year-round residences, in parts of Coney Island. With the coming of the subways and the building of new highways, the increasing accessibility of Coney made it possible, as well as pleasant, to live at the beautiful, breeze-swept shore and commute to work in other parts of the city.

The sturdily built summer houses of Seagate, Manhattan Beach, and Brighton Beach were worth renewing, but the cheaply built summer rental housing which filled West Brighton was not. And so, after World War II, while the first three areas of Coney Island were being re-furbished by and for the middle class, West Brighton continued to deteriorate.

By 1950, the housing shortage in New York City amounted to 430,000 units of decent housing that were needed but not available. The rate of vacancies was the lowest in the United States. For poorly paid working people, and those who were unemployed and on welfare, the need for housing was desperate. It was especially difficult for the new arrivals to the city, the farm workers displaced by mechanization of Southern farms and Puerto Ricans in search of jobs, to find adequate housing.

The shortage of low-rent housing in the city was made more acute, ironically, by a program which had been designed to help the poor. The Federal Government's Housing Act of 1949 called for "the elimination of substandard and other inadequate housing through the clearance of slums and blighted areas and the realization as soon as feasible of the goal of a decent home and a suitable living environment for every American family, thus contributing to the development and re-development of communities."

To carry out this goal, slums in Brooklyn, Manhattan, and the Bronx were bulldozed. The tenants thus made homeless were the low-paid workers, families on welfare, and elderly people on small pensions. Where were they to go?

Welfare workers and relocation agents, searching for low-cost housing, turned to the remaining housing available on Coney Island. The flimsy summer bungalows and rooming houses, clustered along the shabby side streets of West Brighton, were empty in the winter because they lacked heat. The landlords were persuaded to install heating units so that the houses could be used year-round. Twenty-two thousand people, nearly half of them living below the poverty level, were crowded into the area between the middle-income communities of Brighton Beach and Seagate.

According to the New York City Planning Commission: "Even an expensive conversion would have been far from satisfactory but the cheap makeshifts used to make these cottages rentable, coupled with overcrowding . . . have produced abysmal conditions."

Decaying summer bungalows.

The middle-class Coney Island residents were concerned with the spreading blight of poverty into their community. They urged the city leaders to apply for some of the funds made available by the Federal Government Housing Act. In 1954 Gravesend Houses was built for people of limited income, on largely vacant land at the end of West Brighton near Seagate. Fifteen, seven story buildings of dark brick were erected, widely spaced and surrounded by well kept lawns. There are benches for the older people and basketball courts and play-grounds for the young.

The next project to be undertaken by the City Housing Authority was Coney Island Houses built along Surf Avenue, close to the Atlantic Ocean, in 1956. These fourteen story apartment buildings offered attractive, new homes to 534 families. But this housing was for moderate-income tenants. Rents average twice as much as they did in a low-income project, like Gravesend. In moderate-income housing such as Coney Island Houses, only people whose income lies below a figure set by the Housing Authority are eligible to rent apart-ments, but the upper limit is twice as high as it is for those applying to a low-income project.

During the 1950's, and on into the 1960's, New York City's government, as well as governments of other large cities, were finding it difficult to assemble sites on which to build large-scale public housing. So much housing was needed that it was felt only large projects were economic. Poor people, however, as well as middle-class ones, were beginning to protest the destruction of their homes to make way for new housing. And the poor were bitter because so much of the new housing being built was priced beyond their reach. It was often said that the slum clearance program was putting rich people into housing where poor people had lived.

One response to this development was the tightening of federal requirements for relocation of those who were displaced. Before federal funds could be made available for redevelopment, the city had to take the responsibility for seeing that decent housing was provided for those who were evicted. This task became ever more difficult as the clearance of the slums reduced the supply of the necessary cheap rental units.

At this point Coney Island became a very attractive location for public housing. Coney Island had large tracts of empty or sparsely utilized land, the sites of former amusement parks and other relics of the declining summer entertainment industry. Luna Park, in West Brighton, had burned down in 1949 and the city now owned that twenty-four acre site. It was temporarily being used as a parking lot, and presented an ideal opportunity for large scale development for housing; there were no tenants to protest or to relocate.

A low-income housing project was planned and by 1961 the city had built five towering brick apartment houses. It was, architecturally, much more ambitious than the earlier project, Gravesend Houses, or even the moderate-income Coney Island Houses. To take advantage of the beautiful, seaside location, the buildings are laid out in four wings with a terrace for every four apartments. Since this is only two blocks from the ocean, the residents of the four apartments which share each terrace can enjoy the spectacular view and are "Swept by the Ocean Breezes," as the once famous slogan of the old Manhattan Beach Hotel used to proclaim.

Luna Park Houses opened as a low-rent city housing project, and remained so for two years. There were pressures, however, to turn this desirable and attractive area into a middle-income community. The cost of constructing Luna Park Houses was higher than the city had expected, as the price of labor and materials rose. In addition, there were strong community voices, which knew how to reach the ears of powerful political leaders, calling for the up-grading of the buildings and population of Coney Island. The poor were still unorganized and silent.

Two years after Luna Park Houses were built, the city decided to transfer its ownership by turning it into a middle-income cooperative. The apartments were sold to those tenants who could afford the price, which was $500 per room, or to outsiders when vacancies existed. It now became Luna Park Village.

The transformation of a low-income housing project into a middle-income cooperative was financed under a New York State law, the Mitchell-Lama Act of 1955. Senator MacNeil Mitchell and Assemblyman Alfred A. Lama had sponsored this legislation to encourage private builders to put up middle-income housing in the cities, on sites that were either deteriorated or under-utilized. Their purpose was to hold middle-class people in the city, as tax-payers and as a stabilizing political influence. To stem the flight to the suburbs, better housing in the city was offered.

The State and the City Governments were authorized to give developers long term loans for up to fifty years at low interest rates. The city could also offer builders the additional incentive of real estate tax abatements. This meant lowering taxes on the new buildings by assessing the properties at less than they were worth, and by requiring that only a percentage of the taxes needed to be paid during a period of years, up to twenty-five years in some cases, after which the full tax would have to be paid.

Spurred on by the Mitchell-Lama law and the availability of other large tracts of land in West Brighton, developers began to bid for building sites. Between Luna Park and Brighton Beach lay sixty-two acres sparsely filled with small businesses, summer bungalows, and some aging, low-rent housing. Many buildings were boarded up, and others housed poor tenants, some relocated from other rebuilt areas of the city. In all there

Before the building of Trump Village.

were only about five hundred people working or living there, so there was not a great relocation problem.

The first group to put in a bid to the city to redevelop this acreage was the United Housing Foundation, a sponsor of cooperative, largely middle-income, housing. In 1957, they offered to build five thousand housing units with financing under the Mitchell-Lama Act.The apartments would be sold to the tenants, as a middle-income cooperative much like Penn South in Chelsea.

However, in nearby Sheepshead Bay, a private developer, Fred Trump, offered the city an alternative plan. He argued that he could also put up middle-income housing on the site and would pay the city higher taxes. A long drawn out struggle followed. The United Housing Foundation turned for assistance to the politically powerful Amalgamated Clothing Workers Union which had built Penn South. The Trump organization hired skillful and politically astute lawyers. The issue was finally resolved by the city; part of the land was awarded to each group.

The Housing Foundation and the Amalgamated Union cosponsored the development of Warbasse Houses on their 26.7 acres. It took four years to put up five buildings, twenty-four stories high, plus a cooperative shopping center. Over twenty-five hundred families bought apartments, at $850 per room, and became cooperators.

Who were the people who moved into Warbasse Houses and where did they come from? Nearly two thousand moved there from other parts of Coney Island, or from Brooklyn. But none of the 536 families who had lived on the site and had been relocated by the United Housing Foundation, could afford to move back. Almost all of them moved into the crowded low-cost housing in West Brighton, or other parts of Brooklyn.

Across the street from the Warbasse Houses, on the remaining thirty-six acres, the Fred Trump building organization constructed seven tall apartment buildings. Trump Village provided new homes for 3,696 families. Five of the buildings were sold to tenants, as cooperatives, for $450 to $500 per room. The other two houses still belong to the Trump organization and are rental units.

With Luna Park Village, Amalgamated-Warbasse Houses, and Trump Village, Coney Island developed a new skyline. Gone were many of the fanciful towers and minarets of amusement parks and the Victorian gables and turrets of the mammoth summer hotels. Under the stimulus of the Mitchell-Lama financial incentives new, government aided housing was provided for 8,600 middle-class families in Coney Island.

West Brighton—Housing the Lower Third

What was happening to the housing needs of the poor, those who were crowded into the old summer bungalows? The situation of the poor in West Brighton had worsened. The relocation of the families who were displaced to make way for Trump, Luna, and Warbasse Houses added to the crowding in the remaining area of West Brighton. In addition, middle-class families, with few children, moved into the new housing and their former homes were filled by poorer and often larger families.

By the 1960's a twenty-three block section of West Brighton, between the amusement area around Stillwell Avenue and the fence around Seagate, contained twenty thousand people. These people were crowded into old houses, many of them dilapidated. This blight in central Coney Island especially hurt those who lived there, but it also affected the merchants who ran the shops along Mermaid Avenue. Despite their wall, the residents of neighboring Seagate were concerned. The children went to school in West Brighton and the adults had to pass through it on their way to the subway or to shop.

The business and civic groups in the community, which were largely representative of the middle class, came together in 1960 to form the Coney Island Community Council. They were instrumental in persuading the Federal Government to build much needed low-income housing, and plans were drawn up for two such projects, Carey Gardens and Mermaid Houses. The community council urged the city to balance this, to preserve a middle class presence in the community, by putting up middle-income housing. Sam Burt Houses and William O'Dwyer Gardens were to be built to fulfil this objective.

In addition to the housing needs of the poor, the Coney Island Community Council addressed itself to the many other problems which beset this group. In 1965 the Council applied to the Federal Government for an $80,000 grant under the Economic Opportunity Act, to set up a Family Center. The sponsorship and the first Board of Directors were middle class, but the act stipulated that the funds must be spent with "maximum feasible participation of the residents and members of the area served." Within a year the Board of Directors was replaced by a new group which was representative of the poor.

The most urgent problem facing the people in the area served by the Family Center was housing. As they saw thousands of new apartments which they could not afford going up in the community resentment grew. Some of this feeling came to the surface when the Steeplechase Park property went up for sale in 1965. Recreational facilities are in short supply in West Brighton. There is only one playground, Kaiser Park, and that is tucked away near Gravesend Bay. Residents of West Brighton suggested to the city that the Steeplechase site be purchased and used to provide a park for the community. Instead the owners sold their land to the builder, Fred Trump, who proposed to put up a group of middle-income apartment houses along the lines of Trump Village. In order to do so Mr. Trump had to apply to the City Planning Commission for a

Mermaid Houses—where decaying summer bungalows once stood.

zoning variance to permit residential building in what had hitherto been a commercial zone.

The community fought against the granting of the variance, and the City Planning Commission denied it. Blocked from using the site for housing, the Trump organization sold the land to the city. Unfortunately, no money has been made available in the city budget to develop a park on the site.

The urgent need for better housing and the fear of being pushed out by new high-rent buildings united the tenants of West Brighton. One of the leaders whom they elected to the board of the Family Center, Mrs. Sophie Smith, expressed these feelings vividly: "We came here after being pushed out of other areas of the city that were being renewed. This is the end. There's no place for us to go except into the ocean." Those who lived in the terrible housing that was to be razed wanted to stay in their neighborhood and to have housing built there which they could afford. So many had been uprooted before by the bulldozers of renewal, that the poor felt for them renewal meant removal.

The city announced plans for a new type of slum clearance, vest pocket housing. According to this plan, development would occur on sites as small as one acre, that could be quickly assembled, cleared, and rebuilt with little dislocation of people living there. Coney Island was selected as an area suitable for this type of redevelopment, because Carey Gardens and O'Dwyer Gardens were nearing completion and would provide an ideal place to relocate the tenants from new, vest pocket sites.

The spokesmen for the poor, the board of the Family Center, and those who represented the middle class, the Coney Island Community Council, were determined to have a voice in the decisions which were being made for Coney Island. The poor were intent on stopping what they saw as an effort by the middle-class residents of Seagate and the Mitchell-Lama projects, allied with the businessmen of Coney Island, to squeeze them out and build an all high-rise, expensive 'Miami Beach.' "Let them stay behind the Seagate Wall and leave us alone and stop trying to plan for us" said the leaders of the poor.

The middle-class members of the Coney Island Community Council saw the issue differently. They argued that they were not opposed to low-income housing, and had, in fact, urged it on the city. But, they said, if a preponderance of low-income families were brought in, a new vertical slum would take shape. They sought a variety of housing that would appeal to a mixture of rich and poor. The council wanted to rebuild Coney Island by taking advantage of the natural resources of beauty, beaches, and climate. It was difficult for the middle-income leaders to understand the hostility they met from the poor, the rejection of their leadership.

Atkins Preston, who was director of the Family Center in the 1960's, put it this way: "Coney Island will never be quiescent again. It won't ever again be a voiceless area that is being planned around."

The residents served by the Family Center united to make sure that the new vest pocket housing would give priority to their urgent needs. Under their leaders in the Family Center they gathered together the representatives of all their community groups and in 1968 formed a Coordinating Committee.

The Coney Island Community Council, representing the middle class, and the Coordinating Committee of the poor, sought the ear of the City Planning Commission. But who speaks for the community when many conflicting voices are raised?

The representatives of the poor felt that their most convincing argument for new low-cost housing was a first-hand observation of the deplorable conditions that existed in West Brighton. They urged members of the City Planning Commission to come out to Coney Island and to see for themselves.

Several members of the commission made the trip. They walked the garbage-littered streets, lined with dilapidated or gutted buildings. As they entered the houses they were greeted by rats and roaches, as well as tenants. The broken plaster and leaking pipes they saw helped them to understand why the City Housing Department had classified 85 percent of the dwelling units in West Brighton as "sub-standard."

Consulting the Community

The City Planning Commission appointed a young architect, Alex Cooper, to study the problems of Coney Island and to work with all groups in the community in developing a housing plan. Mr. Cooper was chosen because he was known to be sensitively aware of the growing resentment by neighborhood people of outside planning. He described what was happening in the neighborhoods as the evolution of a turf concept. People were claiming that those who lived in an area had a right to affect the decisions that touched their community. They were challenging ownership of land and buildings as the sole consideration in determining change. In the late 1960's the demand for community participation became louder and louder.

In April of 1968 Alex Cooper came out to Coney Island to meet representatives of all factions. Out of this meeting he formed a housing planning committee. Meeting two and three nights a week throughout the summer, the housing committee and Alex Cooper hammered out a Neighborhood Development Plan. They agreed that half of the new housing units were to be for low-income families and half for moderate-income tenants. The plan was presented to the City Planning Commission, which approved it. Then the housing committee selected the sites to be cleared, with emphasis on those which were

Housing the poor in West Brighton.

under-utilized and did not involve the displacement of large numbers of people.

A chain was set up in Coney Island with each new housing project, as it moved to completion, providing good, permanent relocation for the people on the next site which was scheduled to be rebuilt. Plans, cleared sites, housing foundations, and soaring new apartment buildings were stages of neighborhood renewal that became a part of the Coney Island picture.

In the target area, which extends from Stillwell Avenue to Thirty-seventh Street, three thousand units have been or will be built with city, state, or federal money. And when all of these projects are completed, 60 percent of those who were living in substandard dwellings will be living in decent, modern homes.

Not long ago a candidate for Mayor of New York City campaigned on the slogan "Power to the Neighborhoods." He was appealing to the growing number of people who believe that much of the decision making in government should be brought back to the local level. Increasingly, local communities are being consulted by the City Government and are participating in the planning for their area.

Much of this decentralization gives the local community an advisory role but not the decision-making power. For example, all over New York City the Borough Presidents have appointed Community Planning Boards. Their role is to "consider the needs of the districts and develop plans for the district's welfare and orderly development [and] advise any public officer or body with respect to any matter relating to the welfare of the district whether or not advice is requested."

Coney Island's Community Planning Board is made up of businessmen, a nurse, a plumber, and a bus driver, among others. The thirteen members meet for two hours a month to discuss and listen to suggestions for Coney Island. One of the programs they have been urging on the city is the establishment of day care centers. Many of the families in Central Coney

Island are headed by women, and good, dependable supervision of their children would make it possible for these women to take jobs to support their families.

Sometimes the Community Planning Board succeeds in preventing changes which residents do not want from being made in their neighborhood. One of these battles took place over the location in Coney Island of an industrial park which would be reserved for factories, and neatly separated from residential areas. The City Planning Commission proposed to do this along Neptune Avenue where auto repair shops and a knitwear factory were surrounded by groups of neatly kept private homes. The houses were to be torn down and industries from other areas relocated in their place. The residents, however, objected. They urged their community board to fight the plan, and to encourage the choice of another site for an industrial park. The Coney Island Creek area, where there were more factories and fewer homes, was chosen.

In the important field of health care the city has also moved toward community participation. City hospitals have been ordered to set up advisory boards which "will participate in establishing policy at its hospital and shall consider and advise the . . . hospital upon matters concerning the development of plans and programs." The boards must contain a majority of consumers, defined as "those who regularly use the hospital as their primary source of health service."

How has this worked in Coney Island? One of the problems of the poor in Coney Island has been the inaccessibility of their hospital, which lies outside their neighborhood in Gravesend. This has meant they must go to the effort and expense of taking two buses to get to the hospital clinic. The community board sponsored the establishment of a pediatric satellite clinic at a housing project in Central Coney Island. Two afternoons a week doctors and nurses are available there to examine children who are brought in. In its first six months of operation the clinic detected cases of lead poisoning, tuberculosis, and other illnesses and the children who needed treatment were sent to the hospital for it.

The health needs of the many senior citizens on Coney Island also cannot be met by distant Coney Island Hospital. Plans, but so far not funds, are committed to establishing senior clinics. As a beginning, the hospital staff conducts eye screening tests six times a year at Haber Houses, a public housing project for senior citizens on Surf Avenue.

A school decentralization law now puts Coney Island's schools under the supervision of a nine member board of local residents, elected by the people in the community. With the funds it receives from the government, the board must decide which programs will be supported and which they cannot afford. The head of the Community School Board is Mrs. Celia Kushner, and she talks with us about the needs and the resources available to deal with them.

"One of the reasons the young families of people who grew up here moved away was that the schools in this area were old, over-crowded, and some were on double sessions. To make the situation worse, the families who moved in had more children still. With the new housing projects we are getting additional families, large families and we are busing some of these children two miles away to Brighton Beach where there are empty classrooms.

"We know," Mrs. Kushner continues, "that poor children need special help and smaller classes and remedial reading. So we plead with the city for 'More Effective Schools' programs because there are special funds for this. We beg the state for money for programs we know we need, and we compete with all the other schools in the city for the Federal Government's Title I grants for helping underprivileged children. We have responsibility on the Community School Board, and we know what our children need, but we aren't given enough money to do what must be done."

In addition to funding the Family Center, the Federal Government's Office of Economic Opportunity has provided funds for programs designed by the residents to improve their impoverished community. The money is administered by a locally elected group, the Coney Island Community Associates, which also supervises the Family Center.

We visit one of these projects in a store front on Mermaid Avenue. It is called Operation Outreach and is run by Gloria Edwards who lives, with her seven children, in one of the new low-income housing projects, Carey Gardens. "My job is to work with the troubled, low-income family whose child is having trouble with school, or who drops out. Sometimes I find a child is a truant because his family is too poor to provide him with the clothes he needs to attend school. Then I call around to charitable groups until I can get what is needed."

Parents come to Mrs. Edwards for help when their children are suspended, or unable to get along with their teachers. Dealing with school officials may be too much for parents who are timid, or are foreign born and cannot speak English. Mrs. Edwards works especially hard to encourage parents to keep their children in school until they graduate. She also helps teenagers who have dropped out to return to school. She finds jobs, or even homes, for them when necessary.

In Coney Island, as well as in other areas of the city, the Mayor has set up an Urban Task Force. A paid staff is available to help local residents in their relations with government agencies. Doris Hart is a member of the Coney Island Task Force and runs a "Neighborhood City Hall." Into her street level office on Mermaid Avenue stream people with problems. Mrs. Hart and her staff steer them to the right city agency, help them to fill out complicated forms, and listen to their complaints. It is also the job of the Urban Task Force to relay

Coney Island children's playground.

back to the City Government suggestions for improving city services.

Doris Hart has lived in Coney Island for eighteen years and has been a volunteer or paid worker in more community organizations than she can count, including the Community Planning Board. She discusses her neighborhood's many, unsolved problems with us. "We need jobs for the thousands of people on welfare, and day care centers so women with children can go out to work. We need housing, enough housing to take all the people living in those broken down summer bungalows out of them. And we really need more recreation facilities for our teenagers. Now, the only place they can hang out is the pool halls, and that's where the drug pushers operate."

In spite of these problems Mrs. Hart insists that Coney Island is a good place to live and a great place in which to bring up her children. The struggle between different neighborhood groups for control and recognition as *the* spokesman for the community disturbs her most of all.

"I think we're moving together, people beginning to see that each side has some right and some wrong. And we need each other. We've got to talk to each other and find the things we both want." Mrs. Hart sees this happening and is optimistic about the future of her neighborhood, and the spirit of cooperation emerging in her neighbors.

Marcy Feigenbaum, who lives in Trump Village, repeats Mrs. Hart's plea for cooperation among local groups. "If the community goes down to City Hall together, they can win. But if they fight over whose program should be adopted the city will just walk away from the whole problem."

Celia Kushner, in Seagate, agrees cautiously. As she sees it, those who once fought so bitterly for more low-income housing now realize that they do not want their neighborhood to become a segregated poverty pocket. And the champions of more middle-income housing increasingly have come to accept the right of those who live so miserably in the slums of Coney Island, to be re-housed, decently, in their neighborhood. And they recognize that this need is urgent.

The hope for the future of Coney Island is the fierce love by its residents of this neighborhood, their unique seashore on the subway. "Once you get sand in your toes you will never leave" as Walter Fass of Luna Park Houses puts it. And Celia Kushner quotes "If you ever smell the ocean you cannot go away."

Between Seagate and Manhattan Beach residents are organized into over a hundred community organizations. They are concerned about their neighborhood. Doris Hart sees this as a problem—and a promise. "Communication between people and groups in the community has got to be improved. We have to work at that so we can work with each other. And if the different organizations will then get together, this place could be beautiful."

In the neighboring borough of Queens there is another community struggling to renew itself whose motto is "Progress through all peoples working together." That neighborhood is Jamaica Center, a declining business district. Let's see what community cooperation has actually accomplished.

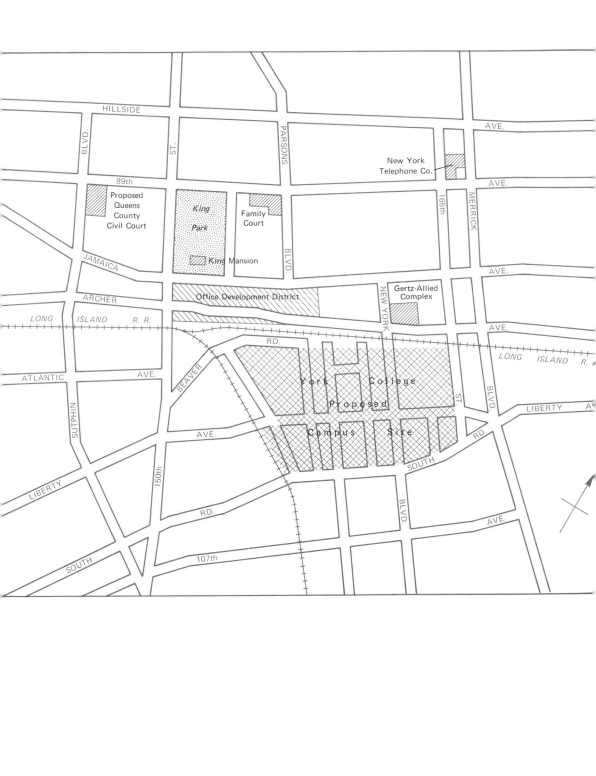

PART THREE

JAMAICA

Renewal of a "Downtown"

Time Present—Time Past

We have come to Jamaica, Long Island to study the revival of a neighborhood quite different from Chelsea and Coney Island. It is a business district and the fight to renew it has been led by businessmen, those who earn their livelihood in the community. And so we shall take our first walk along the main business artery, Jamaica Avenue.

Our impression is a gloomy one ideed, for the street is over-shadowed and darkened by the antiquated mass transit structure overhead, the el. On the street level buses, trucks, and autos inch their way between the pillars that support the el, amid a bedlam of noise and confusion.

We start our stroll on a corner where there is a large department store with attractive displays in its windows. Almost immediately we come upon shoddy little shops cluttered with cheap merchandise: hats, shoes, lamps, furniture, and discount wigs. Bold signs advertise such attractions as "Sister Susie—Reader, Adviser." Here you can come and have your fortune told.

There is a movie house on Jamaica Avenue whose old facade bears only traces of a gayer, brighter day. People scurry

Jamaica Avenue—the shadow of the el.

by; women with their shopping bags, young people licking ice cream cones, a few students with books under their arms.

Suddenly, an abrupt break in the endless line of stores brings us back to the 18th century. Before us stands a beautiful old church, the Grace Episcopal, completely surrounded by ancient, worn gravestones whose dates were chiseled in the 1700's.

A few more steps along the avenue and we are back in the present, jostled by the crowds of shoppers, too many for the narrow sidewalk. After several more blocks of small retail businesses there is another welcome change. A large, block-square park stands quietly in the midst of Jamaica Avenue's bustle. Trees, lawns, and benches surround a large, white colonial mansion. This was the home of Rufus King, Jamaica's leading citizen in a bygone day. King was New York's first senator, and our nation's first ambassador to Great Britain.

The King Mansion is preserved now as an historic landmark, but not well-preserved to judge by its appearance. The benches, however, seem to provide a welcome resting place for the shoppers.

Across from the park is an old department store building with a freshly painted sign, "York College," and students are standing in small clusters near its doors.

Churches, the park, and the temporary college headquarters are but brief interruptions in the long line of small retail shops. Many of the stores are substantially built and well-stocked, while others display their cheaper wares on sidewalk stands. Lunchrooms and food shops add their pungent odors to the fumes from the dense auto traffic. More depressing are the vacant, boarded store windows which are interspersed among the others. And the ever-present eyesore overhead, from which comes the periodic, nerve-shattering rumble of the el trains, makes Jamaica Avenue a most depressing scene.

The King Mansion in 1971.

Is it possible to save and rebuild an area like this? Is it worth saving?

Let's roll back the calendar to the beginning of Jamaica as a white man's settlement. The story opens in 1644 with a party of English Presbyterians who founded the village of Heemsteede (today called Hempstead) on the fertile inland plain directly across Long Island Sound from Connecticut. These settlers had migrated from Stamford, Connecticut because of the hostility of their Puritan neighbors. They also felt crowded there and yearned for more land to farm.

In 1655 a small group of these "inhabitense of Heemsteede" set out to found a still newer town. Once again they felt themselves hemmed in and sought greener pastures. About ten miles west of Hempstead they found land to their liking on the broad slope which ran south from "the Hills" to a large and sparkling bay.

The Canarsie Indians who had lived there before them had called this area Ahmeco or Yameco after the beavers who built their dams in the neighboring creeks and ponds. An Anglicized version—Jamaica—was the name finally chosen for the fast-growing village when the British triumphed over the Dutch in 1664.

The English villagers were gradually joined, in the 1680's, by Dutch families who began to purchase land in Jamaica and to build homesteads and cultivate their farms in and around the little town.

"All matters of concernment" to the community were dealt with at public town meetings. Every villager was ordered to attend, on threat of fine. An early act cautioned all citizens "to do nothing that shall in any ways be prejudicial to their neighbors."

The land of Long Island purchased, or more accurately, seized, from the Indians, had been covered for centuries with vegetable mould which enriched the soil. The mild, maritime climate brought Spring earlier and held Autumn later than areas at the same latitude further inland. Thus physiography, climate, and location combined to make Long Island one of the richest and eventually one of the most important garden spots in the United States.

Long Island agriculture of the seventeenth and eighteenth centuries was characterized by well-managed, self-sufficient farms. By the beginning of the nineteenth century the farmers of Jamaica were growing subsistence crops and in addition a surplus which they sold. At the same time transportation was steadily improving. Mud-prone dirt roads were being covered with wooden planks, making them more serviceable. There were also boats and ferries traveling the East River and supplying the waterfront markets in Manhattan and Brooklyn. The Erie Canal, completed in 1825, was providing a cheaper way to send the products of the East to the new markets in the expanding West.

The opening of Long Island to rail transportation, in 1836, made it possible for the farmers there to switch from grain and cattle production to potato growing and market gardening. This second type of agriculture, the intensive cultivation of perishable vegetables and fruits, was dependent on quick marketing and brought far higher returns per acre than the cereal crops. Large farms were gradually divided into smaller units as owners turned to growing lettuce, spinach, cabbage, and melon.

Farmers who were able to go to market in their wagons used Jamaica Avenue as their main thoroughfare. The horse-drawn vehicles groaned under the weight of garden-fresh produce on its way to the ever-growing population of the central parts of New York City.

On their way home again the weary farmers would stop in Jamaica to rest themselves and their horses. With cash in their pockets, the farmers bought cookstoves or new boots for the family, and all the household necessities which were available in Jamaica's well-stocked stores.

A major factor in the growth of Jamaica's prospering retail business was the continuing advance of public transportation. In the last decades of the nineteenth century bridges were built to span the East River so that traffic between Manhattan and Long Island was no longer dependent on boats and the weather. Roads and thoroughfares multiplied. The first years of the 1900's saw the completion of an overhead rapid transit system from Manhattan, the central city, to an end terminal on Jamaica Avenue. During this period the Long Island Rail Road added a network of lines over the entire island, and all but one of them passed through Jamaica, a transfer point for passengers. "Change at Jamaica" the conductors shouted, and many years later this was to become the rallying cry of citizens working to improve their community.

The expanding system of transportation not only followed growth, but as in Chelsea and Coney Island, it stimulated development. As the central city became more and more crowded, people who worked there moved farther and farther out in their search for cheaper land on which to build homes. Public transportation made this exodus possible, by enabling workers to commute rapidly from Jamaica to Manhattan.

As families crowded into Jamaica and its environs, the loose farm road patterns gave way to a denser configuration of streets and avenues which made subdivision of land easier. Thus, remaining large farms were broken up and gradually the smaller market gardens were replaced by row after row of modest one and two-family houses, with little front and back yards. Many of the new residents traveled to other parts of the city to work. Some found jobs in the factories springing up around Newtown Creek, across the East River from Manhattan.

Most of Long Island's traffic, both passenger and commercial, continued to pass through Jamaica. Geography fa-

Jamaica Avenue, 1800.

Jamaica Avenue, now.

vored the area, as it had in earlier days. Location continued to encourage Jamaica's development as a focal point for retail business.

Jamaica Avenue was the busiest street, lined with shops that catered to the many people flowing by. The elevated railroad was considered a great advance when it was first built. It separated the various streams of traffic, carrying passengers on the trains high above and leaving the street for pedestrians and vehicles. Although the heavy structure cast dark shadows on the stores, it also helped bring thousands of customers to them.

Heyday and Decline

In the early years of the twentieth century, if an enterprising individual were looking for a place to start a small business, he could do little better than to choose Jamaica. It was a pleasant town with a stately courthouse, a splendid network of transportation facilities, and many substantial residences. It was a neighborhood whose more distant outskirts were still surrounded by large farms and fine estates. Furthermore, Jamaica was situated in the middle of the thriving, fast-growing Borough of Queens, which had become a part of Greater New York in 1898. The borough boasted a population of more than a quarter million at the turn of the century.

The story of one man's success as a neighborhood merchant illustrates Jamaica's growth as a business center. In 1911 middle-aged Benjamin Gertz brought his wife, their daughter, and four sons to Jamaica from Brooklyn to seek their fortunes. Mr. Gertz, born in Poland, had started his life in America as a boy of nineteen on New York's lower East Side.

After some searching Benjamin Gertz found a location and opened a small stationery store on Jamaica Avenue. The place was not much to look at, but it was soon the scene of a lively business in newspapers, magazines, school supplies, and tobacco. Ben Gertz was assisted by his wife, daughter, and son-in-law; the enterprise was quite a family affair. With its friendly atmosphere, the small store became a popular spot for young and old.

In five years the Gertz family moved its store to a larger one across the street. The four sons all went to college and eventually became involved in the family's thriving business.

New types of merchandise were constantly added, starting with cameras, sporting goods, fountain pens, and sheet music. Next came phonographs, records, and even those newly invented radios.

In 1924 Gertz occupied a three story building on Jamaica Avenue; four years later a six story wing was added. Leather goods, boys' wear, umbrellas, and jewelry were soon on display. These were followed by cosmetics, fabrics, and a photographic studio.

By 1931, just twenty years after the family's move to Jamaica, their business transformation was complete. "Gertz" had grown from a tiny stationery store to one of the largest department stores in the City of New York. When Benjamin Gertz died in 1933, his establishment was well known on Long Island; a monument, people called it, to his faith in Jamaica.

The department store and the rest of Jamaica's business community, including theatres and a race track, prospered as population in the central city overflowed into Queens and then beyond into the adjoining counties, Nassau and Suffolk. By 1940 over half a million people did their shopping in Jamaica. It became the third largest retail center in the whole New York Metropolitan Region.

Mass transportation continued to serve Jamaica well. A new subway, underground this time, was built in 1937, and brought people within easy walking distance of the main shopping area.

**Misspelled beginning of the third largest retail center in New
York. The sign maker made a mistake.**

Fanning out from the subway, elevated, and railroad were sixteen bus lines whose thousands of motor coaches carried passengers from the stations to all parts of Queens, and brought shoppers to Jamaica's stores.

Jamaica was "downtown" for the adjoining residential communities. North of Jamaica Avenue, where the new subway ran underground, was a neatly-kept neighborhood of large and small private homes. Apartment houses began to appear in the 1930's, and more and more were built along the path of the new subway. A substantial group of middle-class, white-collar workers was attracted to the area.

To the south of Jamaica Avenue, separated from it by the tracks of the Long Island Rail Road and a sprawling industrial strip, more modest houses were built in the 1920's. Developers put up inexpensive, small one and two-family houses. They offered a step up to low-paid workers who sought to escape from the crowded, decaying tenements of Brooklyn and Manhattan. They were priced within the reach of the working poor, and offered them an opportunity to become owners rather than renters. Thus, the houses were owner-occupied and cared for, and the families who lived in them were customers for Jamaica's busy merchants.

After World War II, people searching for homes came to Queens. The Federal Housing Authority was lending home buyers money, on easy terms, to encourage private residential construction. The government was also building highways that made it increasingly easy for car owners to work a distance from their homes. Both these forces spurred the move to the fringes of cities and beyond, away from old housing and crowded streets. By 1960 nearly a million people were living within a thirty minute travel radius of Jamaica's market area.

Population growth did not stop in Queens. It spread even more rapidly to the adjacent counties of Nassau and Suffolk. Land was cheaper as one went farther out, and the network of

Residential Jamaica.

expanding highways made more distant locations increasingly accessible. Therefore, not all of this growth added to Jamaica's prosperity.

As people migrated farther out on Long Island, new rivals for Jamaica's traditional retail role developed. David Lutin, a regional planner, describes what happened: "The decline of Jamaica which before World War II was the dominant shopping and entertainment center of Long Island, originated with the advent of new shopping centers in nearby Nassau County and worsened in recent years under the competitive impact of newer shopping centers in Queens. This business erosion is reflected by vacant stores, dingy, deteriorating, and obsolescent buildings, closed movie theaters—Jamaica retailers have lost about one-fourth of their customers to Nassau County shopping centers and large numbers of new stores elsewhere in Queens. The situation is aggravated further by traffic congestion and parking difficulties."

Jamaica's businessmen, who had prospered with a clientele that was a mixture of middle and lower middle-class customers, began to see the change reflected in their stores. Many of the prosperous, who owned cars, were finding it more convenient and pleasant to drive to outlying shopping centers, where highways were less crowded and parking was readily available.

Responding to the challenge of the growing competition, some stores in Jamaica were remodeled and made more attractive, with new fixtures and lighting. But many of them remained cramped and old-fashioned because their owners were unwilling to modernize, or could not afford to do so.

The merchants in Jamaica became increasingly dependent on those who lived nearby, and some of these local residents were people with little money to spend. As the area south of the business district grew older, especially after 1950, the houses changed hands. Owner-tenants who had prospered moved out to bigger homes or newer housing developments. Some of the buildings they left were then converted into multi-family units or rooming houses.

The cheaply built structures deteriorated. Plaster walls cracked, cheap plumbing broke down, and electrical wiring designed to carry the load of a single family's appliances was inadequate under the strain of several users.

It costs money to make the repairs which are frequently necessary in such shoddily built and overworked houses. When the New York City Housing and Development Administration did a survey in the area in the 1960's, they found that more than a third of the families "have incomes under the poverty line standard of $5,000 a year for a family of four."

As you walk down the residential streets of this neighborhood, south of Jamaica Avenue and beyond the Long Island Rail Road tracks, it is easy to spot the owner-occupied homes. They are small, but neat and lovingly maintained. Interspersed among them are some houses which are neglected and overcrowded, with broken or boarded up windows. The wooden steps sag, the porches are littered, and the front yards are piled with discarded and broken household objects.

The Businessmen Take Hold

The businessmen of Jamaica became alarmed at what they saw shaping up for them in the years ahead—fewer and poorer customers. They began to consult with each other, especially in their strong civic association, the Jamaica Chamber of Commerce.

Remember the town meetings which the early settlers held to deal with "all matters of concernment"? The later Jamaicans discussed their mutual problems at meetings of their Chamber of Commerce with its eight hundred members. They soon

Residential Jamaica.

realized that they were faced with a situation which no in-dividual could substantially improve. Their next step was to decide to put their efforts together, to pool their resources and seek a solution.

In 1961, the Chamber of Commerce set up an Urban Renewal Steering Committee to explore the possibilities for rebuilding the blighted areas in their neighborhood and taking other steps toward making Jamaica more attractive to cus-tomers. They hired an urban planning firm to advise them.

These consultants, the first of many, studied the area and in October, 1961 came up with the suggestion that effective action could be initiated best by the preparation of a plan for the overall area.

A report spelled out the problems—and potential—of downtown Jamaica. The retail center, with more than a thou-sand commercial enterprises, had an annual sales volume of over $350,000,000. But the heart of the shopping area, Jamaica Avenue, was declining. If Jamaica was to retain its middle-class clientele and take advantage of the population growth in its market area, the central business district would have to be made more attractive.

Take down the old, gloomy el and put the subway tracks underground, the report suggested. Close the side streets to automobile traffic and turn some of them into pedestrian malls with tree shaded benches, to make shopping pleasureable.

In addition, the planners pointed out that parking facilities must be increased to lure car-driving shoppers back to Jamai-ca. The city must be persuaded to build several multi-storied garages, providing at least four thousand spaces. Some should be placed near the subways and the railroad, for commuters who need all-day parking; others should be placed near the retail center for the convenience of shoppers and business-men.

The report also suggested that Jamaica seek federal funds

Jamaica el—the end of the line.

to redevelop its most deteriorated section, the 110 acres adjacent to the Long Island Rail Road tracks. This area lay between the business district and the residential community to the south.

Empty lots, junkyards, and decaying factories were the principal features of the site. But this under-utilized land was potentially valuable; its location near excellent transportation made it worth developing. The planners felt it could be renewed as a modern industrial park and center for office buildings. The enhancement of a run-down area and the bringing of new jobs and additional customers would benefit both residents and businessmen in the community.

When the report was presented to the residents of the community they reacted angrily to the proposal. Although lack of jobs was a serious problem for people in the poor neighborhood, and the proposed redevelopment would create new employment opportunities, that consideration was not enough to convince the residents. They had not been consulted by the consultants; only the businessmen had been.

The planners' proposal had only taken into account the wishes and suggestions of one group in the neighborhood; the businessmen. As one member of the Chamber of Commerce described the result, "We had an open meeting for both groups and the residential community shot the plan down. They didn't see any improvement for their neighborhood coming out of an industrial park." And so nothing was done; the report gathered dust on a shelf at the chamber's office and the area continued to decay, blighting both the business center and the adjoining residential community.

After burying its dead plan, the Chamber of Commerce decided to build on new, sturdier foundations. The businessmen realized that their longed-for renewal of Jamaica Center could only be brought about through the efforts of a united community. Their first step in this direction was to establish a

Civil Rights Council "to assist in helping solve problems confronting our community and to maintain open dialogue and understanding among all peoples in Jamaica."

The original membership of the council was made up of twenty representatives of local organizations. The name of the council was eventually changed, to the Human Resources Council and its membership grew to ninety-four, representing every important group in both the residential and business community.

Meeting every month to discuss problems as they arose in the community, the Human Resources Council dedicated itself to working to find solutions that would benefit all of the people in Jamaica. They found three areas that were of particular concern to the residential community: drug abuse, unemployment, and the lack of recreational facilities.

To help those with limited education find employment, the Chamber of Commerce, urged on by the council, undertook to sponsor an On the Job Training Program. The chamber entered into a contract with the Federal Government to provide job opportunities, through cooperation with employers who would undertake to train the unskilled. Over 1,000 people have been in the program which pays workers while they are learning, and subsidizes Jamaica businessmen while they act as teacher-employers. This program has been so successful that it has been expanded each year since its inception.

The Human Resources Council has also encouraged and supported the efforts of those in the community attempting to cope with the drug addiction problem. A local doctor and some former addicts proposed to run a sorely needed treatment center. They came to the Human Resources Council for help. The council was able to get these people the use of an empty garage. The young people were willing to transform it into a pleasant and efficient facility, but they had no money for materials. The businessmen of Jamaica helped them overcome

On the Job Training Program, 1966.

this hurdle by donating the paint, lumber, and tools which were needed.

For the children of the neighboring area, each year the Chamber of Commerce has organized recreational and entertainment programs. Tens of thousands of free tickets to Yankee and Mets baseball games are distributed. When the circus comes to town in the Spring, busloads of Jamaica children are treated to it. And the chamber's sponsorship has paid a professional basketball player to conduct basketball training clinics in playgrounds throughout the Southeast Queens community.

The many projects aimed at making Jamaica a better place to live and work established a new foundation for cooperation in the community. As Richard White, the executive director of the Chamber of Commerce, put it, "Before we could get any development we had to have rapport between all the people, to get them working hand in hand. We have learned that we never make a move unless the community is informed and goes along. It can't be 'us' and 'them'; it has to be we!"

The need for improvements in transportation was recognized by all groups in the community. The businessmen wanted the gloomy el removed from Jamaica Avenue, and the residents of Southeast Queens were eager to have a subway extended out to their area. Both of these objectives could be achieved if the city were convinced that an overall program to revitalize Jamaica was needed. The community leaders and spokesmen brought a plan to the New York City and state agencies which had the power to implement it. They came with the support and endorsement of civic organizations. Government officials listened, and were impressed by the political strength of this neighborhood which was strongly organized and spoke out with a single voice.

The chairman of the Metropolitan Transportation Authority agreed to join their advisory committee. During the next six years most of the transportation proposals were adopted, scheduled, and budgeted. In August of 1972 the Governor and the Mayor manned jackhammer drills to begin construction of the new subway!

The businessmen of Jamaica continued their search for ways to revitalize the decaying business district. Committees were formed to visit other cities with similar problems and to consult private and governmental agencies concerned with urban development. What kinds of changes, they asked, will enable an old commercial area to compete with both the new rivals in the suburbs and the magnetic central business district in Manhattan?

Sub-Center versus Spread City

In 1966 the fifty-year-old Regional Plan Association—a group of private citizens dedicated to working for the efficient and attractive development of the metropolitan region surrounding the Port of New York—invited two Jamaicans, the editor of the *Long Island Press* and the president of Queens College, to serve on its advisory board. The association was then at work on a plan to strengthen "emerging centers in the metropolitan area as a desirable alternative to continued unchecked expansion" which was leading to "Spread City," a haphazard development of unrelated offices, shopping centers, and factories in the outlying suburbs. These scattered facilities cannot be served efficiently by a mass transit system. The result is that vacant land must be used for more highways and parking lots since people will be forced to commute to their jobs by automobile.

The plan specifically suggested three prime examples of potential sub-centers to be expanded: Jamaica was one of these. Strengthened and revitalized, these areas should become the "downtown" for a sizeable segment of the region's population.

Jamaica's leaders were delighted with the association's recommendation. They were eager to bring about the necessary changes and turned to the Regional Plan Association for advice. First, they were told, it was necessary to make an up-to-date assessment of Jamaica's problems and possibilities. The Chamber of Commerce agreed, and hired a new urban consultant to do a thorough study.

After several months of investigation and consultation with members of the community, a report was presented to the Chamber of Commerce. It urged the improvement of the subways and their extension into Southeast Queens. The removal of the old el was also recommended, but this time all of the transportation needs of Jamaica were woven into an ambitious plan for coordinating mass transit facilities into an efficient system.

The second important goal suggested by the report was to concentrate on attracting business to Jamaica. The future of the region lay in white collar, office employment. Jamaica could attract the overflow from the central city business district, the office buildings that would otherwise go to scattered outlying areas or locations outside the New York Metropolitan Region.

What would attract potential office builders and tenants to Jamaica rather than to the suburbs or the central city? For one thing rents could be competitively lower, since land costs were lower. In addition, Jamaica could offer employers a large pool of white-collar workers who, thanks to the mass transit facilities, lived within a thirty minute radius. The development of Jamaica as an office center had not happened, despite these arguments in its favor, because Jamaica's image as a declining, old-fashioned retail center was unattractive to investors. The image could be changed by persuading the city to locate new civic institutions there. Jamaica could be the site of a new medical center, a cultural center, and perhaps a new branch of the City University.

There was something in the plan for both groups in the community: opportunities for employment for the residents; thousands of new customers for the merchants. And people who lived in the residential areas of Jamaica were particularly in favor of locating a college in their community.

Soon after the report was finished, the Chamber of Commerce commissioned the Regional Plan Association to do a detailed study of all the implications of the sub-center idea for Jamaica. In 1968, when the association completed its study entitled "Jamaica Center," a delegation of businessmen and community representatives from the Human Relations Council presented the report to the Mayor of New York City, John Lindsay, and to the chairman of the City Planning Commission. The chairman was impressed by the efforts of the community and told the delegates that in view of what the community had done for itself, it would be outrageous if the city didn't step in and lend a helping hand. In fact, the City Planning Commission agreed to make economic, land-use, and transportation studies to test whether the suggestions made in the report could be carried out.

York College

The Jamaica Community now had plans, and a community that was united behind them. The eight hundred members of the Chamber of Commerce had, with the residential community, forged the Human Relations Council to ensure that goals were mutually agreed upon. Now another committee was formed to see that the goals were implemented. It was called the Greater Jamaica Development Corporation.

JAMAICA CENTER
DEVELOPMENT PLAN

OFFICE OF JAMAICA PLANNING AND DEVELOPMENT • QUEENS OFFICE, NYC DEPARTMENT OF CITY PLANNING • GREATER JAMAICA DEVELOPMENT CORPORATION • HART-KRIVATSY-STUBEE, PLANNING CONSULTANTS

Plan for Jamaica Center.

One of the objectives which was important to both groups in the community was the dream of bringing a college to Jamaica. The parents with limited incomes who lived nearby saw it as a ladder to help their children move upward in society. The businessmen were sure that such a cultural institution was a key to the transformation of Jamaica's image.

In 1966 a new branch of the City University was founded and named York College, but its permanent location was not immediately determined. It was temporarily located at Queensborough College, in Bayside, Queens, while the city struggled to decide on its permanent home. Leaders in many parts of the city were vying for the college to be placed in their community.

The united Jamaica community went after the prize. They marshalled the support of the local newspapers, their congressional and borough leaders, and every civic and business organization in the neighborhood. The development corporation produced statistics that showed the city that the students least served by colleges in New York were those in Queens and Brooklyn, and that Jamaica's network of mass transportation made it uniquely accessible to residents of both these boroughs.

One of their most telling arguments was that the location of a city college near a troubled, low-income neighborhood, like the one south of Jamaica Center, would help the area youth to climb up out of poverty. Putting York College on the run-down site near the Long Island Rail Road tracks between the decaying business center and the declining residential area, as the Jamaicans proposed, would thus be a doubly effective use of government funds. It would help uplift two troubled sections of the neighborhood.

The fifty acre site which was proposed for the college was occupied by scattered, dingy industrial and commercial buildings, a cemetery, and a few parking lots. There were not many homes, so that the land could be quickly cleared; few people would need to be relocated.

Having fought for York College together, the residential and business communities celebrated in May of 1968 when the city announced that the new campus would be built in Jamaica. Architects were engaged by the city to draw up plans for a handsome, modern college campus to eventually accommodate 6,000 students. The State Board of Regents agreed to raise the funds, some sixty-two and a half million dollars. Into the open design and landscaping of the campus the planners tried to build an idea; the college as an integral part of the life of the neighborhood. York College was meant to serve as a gateway for the residential community into the larger world, a bridge linking it to Jamaica Center. Instead of walls separating the college from the community, there would be walkways encouraging neighborhood residents to come into, and wander through, the campus.

Under a new city educational policy, open admissions, the college could reach out to help disadvantaged students in the community. This program states that any graduate of a New York City high school is eligible for admission to a city college, even if his or her grades are poor. Since tuition in the city's colleges is free it adds up to the promise that any young person who wants a chance to lift himself out of poverty, through education, can have it.

Even before the new campus could be built, York College moved to takes its place in Jamaica. A former department store building on Jamaica Avenue was taken over and renovated to serve as a temporary headquarters. Twenty-seven hundred students were enrolled in 1971, and 20 percent of them were from Jamaica.

We met with some of the students at York College. Walter, who lives in the neighboring community, was one of them. "I'm twenty-six years old and this is my first and only chance to go to college. But York isn't the complete answer for us. And it's not going to help us unless it is to be the *whole thing*—better elementary schools, a better high school, better housing, a better chance for jobs. York is only a start as far as my people are concerned."

Another student, Rafael, said sadly, "I wanted a beautiful college in a beautiful country place and here we are in Jamaica, in a city slum."

"It's not the place that matters; it's the people" protested a third member of the student group, "and the people here are great!" The others nodded, and agreed, longingly, that things would be better when the new campus was built.

Full Steam Ahead

The York College victory spurred on the Greater Jamaica Development Corporation in its efforts to build a renewed "downtown in town." The businessmen of Jamaica raised money to hire a full-time, professional staff to work toward the goals set forth in the Jamaica Center report.

By December of 1969, the City Planning Commission had completed its feasibility studies of Jamaica's potential and a decision was made "to encourage the rebuilding of sections of downtown Jamaica, to enhance its character as a multi-function metropolitan sub-center for commercial, governmental and institutional activities in the Borough of Queens."

Each step forward in Jamaica's progress helped to gain support for another. The Department of City Planning moved to establish a special Office Development District in downtown Jamaica. It is a ten acre site on which private builders are given special incentives to induce them to build office buildings there.

Site of York College.

The Metropolitan Transportation Authority adopted plans to build the long awaited subway to serve Southeast Queens. And these plans include provisions for station stops to serve the proposed office center and the new York College. The MTA also promised that when the new line was built, the old elevated structure blighting Jamaica Avenue could, at last, be taken down! The final transportation boost to the revitalization of Jamaica was a decision by the city that a planned direct service rail line from Manhattan to Kennedy Airport would include a stop in Jamaica.

A new Family Court and Queens County Civil Court were to be built by the city. The Greater Jamaica Development Corporation worked with the Queens Bar Association to persuade the city that these should be located in Jamaica. Their aim was to strengthen the position of Jamaica as the legal center of the borough. The head of the Queens Bar Association told the Planning Commission, "We are very much in favor of the idea of a complete city, state and federal court complex in the Jamaica area." The decision was made to build the two courthouses in Jamaica.

All together, the commitments to improve Jamaica now added up to 270 million dollars. The Mayor of New York City decided it was important to have all the agencies and programs centrally coordinated, and in 1969 set up an Office of Jamaica Planning and Development. The director was given the power to create an overall plan for the Jamaica area, including both the business neighborhood and the nearby residential community as well. He was to coordinate all city agencies, private interests, and community groups in connection with the plan.

After the city moved to acquire and clear the ten acre special Office Development District, a large real estate developer entered into an agreement with the city to lease two and a half acres. On it he proposed to erect a twenty story office tower, with a shopping plaza at ground level. Near the development site the New York Telephone Company proceeded to construct its new Queens headquarters, housing 1,000 office workers.

"The Bandwagon Is Rolling For A New Jamaica," the *Long Island Press* proclaimed. And Mayor Lindsay told newspaper reporters: "Stanley and Gerald Gertz and Allied Stores have announced they will erect a new high-rise building in the heart of the business district." An office tower, which would be the tallest structure in Jamaica, would be combined with a parking garage and retail stores.

The chairman of the Planning Commission hailed these developments and praised those who had worked to bring them about. "This is a perfect example of public coordination and private initiative. The city could not invest $100 million to strengthen the business community. But we will be spending $100 million for York College, the Civil Court and Family Court as our contribution to this plan. We have created a new investment bandwagon."

That was the mood of optimism, of growing momentum in 1969 and 1970. In its 1971 report the Greater Jamaica Development Corporation talked of arresting the decline and breaking the downward cycle.

The key building blocks in the plans for a renewed Jamaica are York College and the Office Development District. The construction of a beautiful campus would enhance the community physically and enrich it, culturally. York College, the planners maintained, would help make Jamaica attractive to potential office builders and to prospective tenants. Economists were projecting a growth of 235,000 office jobs in the metropolitan region, outside the central city, by the year 2000. Of these, said the Regional Plan Association, the location of 100,000 in Jamaica ought to be the target, however ambitious.

Slow Down or Full Stop?

1971 was a year of economic change. The word recession was used to describe the market place. Unemployment increased as business decreased. The many new office buildings that had gone up in Manhattan during the booming sixties were, suddenly, hard to rent.

Attracting investors to build still more offices, in unproved Jamaica, became difficult. Except for the original two and a half acre lease, the Office Development District's land remained uncommitted. The planned Gertz-Allied complex of stores, garage, and office tower was scaled down. Until rental tenants could be found the office tower would not be built. The garage was urgently needed because the store's parking space had been taken over for York College's new campus-to-be, and it would be built. The ground floor retail stores would also be built, and their foundations would be made strong enough to support the planned office structure. If and when it became economically feasible the office tower would be added.

The weakness of the economy was also affecting the thinking of the State Government. New York State, in 1971, faced a budget deficit as social needs increased and tax revenues declined. Nevertheless the people of Jamaica were not at all prepared for the headline in the *New York Times* on January 1, 1972: "College Plan For Queens Is Rejected."

The Governor, citing the state fiscal crisis, rejected plans for the new campus of York College. The news burst, like sudden death, on the Jamaica community and the college. All those who had labored for ten years to rebuild Jamaica, gathered to fight back.

The Mayor's office announced that the "members of his staff planned to meet with representatives of the Governor to try to work out means of restoring the money." The Queens Borough President called a meeting of the Queens members of the State Legislature to work for the restoration of the promised funds. The Chamber of Commerce, the residential community, and student groups from York College came together to plan protests against the Governor's decision.

The Regional Plan Association held a meeting at York College to discuss the steps that might be taken to persuade the Governor to change his mind, to make him realize the implications of his action.

We asked a leader of the State Legislature if the York College building program was, indeed, dead. "Oh, no" he protested, "it's just been 'rolled over.' Wait a few years. It will be built. But not now."

David Starr, editor of the influential local paper, The *Long Island Press* disputed this judgement. "The City has allocated the million dollars that is needed at this stage to draw up the plans for York College. It is proceeding and it will be built on schedule. The Governor's decision will be reversed before the rest of the money is needed."

Throughout the first half of 1972 the battle for York College continued. The president of the college wrote a letter of appreciation to the *New York Times* for the many friends in the community who were supporting the struggle. "The Governor has disapproved the master plan which would provide a permanent campus . . . Yet even with this dark prospect there is much that is heart-warming. Thousands of our immediate neighbors, the residents of the Jamaica community, have rallied to York's defense . . . Beyond this, an army of supporters has spontaneously arisen throughout the borough—an army that cuts across all partisan lines: it is interfaith, interracial, interethnic and includes the business community, religious and civic leaders and members of all political parties. With so much support from such true friends, I know we will not fail."

In June of 1972 there was a first glimmer of hope for York

College in a letter from David Starr of the *Long Island Press*: "It's still not official, but we have a letter from [Governor] Rockefeller demonstrating that York approval is on the way." The news story in the *Press* attributed the Governor's change of heart to "pressure applied by Mayor Lindsay, Manes [Borough President of Queens] and members of the student body and surrounding communities."

On August 9, 1972 headlines in the local paper brought to the Jamaica community the news they had worked for and waited for since January 1 of that year. The happy headline was "York College: All Systems Are Go." The accompanying story in the *Long Island Press* explained: "With the disclosure yesterday that Governor Rockefeller has given the college master plan his long awaited go-ahead York officials are preparing to hire architects to start planning a new 50 acre campus in the heart of Jamaica."

The very next week the Governor, the Mayor, and hundreds of well-wishers gathered in Jamaica for another important step in the renewal program. Ground was to be broken for the new subway which would serve Southeast Queens and replace the antiquated el over Jamaica Avenue. It was a time of rejoicing and speech making, for celebrating progress and assigning credit.

Mayor Lindsay summed up what had been accomplished: "The momentum builds up, York College is back on the track; the municipal parking garage is well into construction; the new Family Court was dedicated this Spring while the Civil Court is soon to enter the design phase; sponsors are being screened for ten early action housing sites in South Jamaica, and development of commercial and retail space is in various stages ranging from the completed New York Telephone building to the soon to be completed Gertz-Allied retail space to the over 500,000 square feet of commercial space now in final design."

A plan for York College campus.

The Governor predicted: "The old cry of 'Change at Jamaica' is now going to have a new ring to it. The changing Jamaica Avenue of tomorrow will be the hub of civic, educational, business and transportation activity."

The Jamaicans have used community organization, planning, and money to bring about the partnership that was needed to save their neighborhood, a partnership of government, business, and those who live in the community. Their example can help other decaying urban centers to rebuild.

Jamaica's strenuous efforts have attracted the attention of two groups which are dedicated to the cause of saving the cities. The Municipal Arts Society, in 1971, selected the Greater Jamaica Development Corporation and its ally, the South Jamaica Steering Committee, for awards because "their efforts demonstrate in a highly visible form that the city can and will survive the desperate problems that now daily beset it."

Then, in 1972 the National Municipal League named Jamaica its "All-American City." This was the first time the award had been given to a neighborhood rather than to a whole city. The award is designed to "encourage citizens to take the initiative for local improvement."

Mayor John Lindsay had no doubt about the influence Jamaica would have on other citizens and other neighborhoods throughout America. In accepting the municipal league award he put it very forcefully: "The fight for Jamaica is the fight for all the nation's cities. If Jamaica Avenue cannot be saved, Fifth Avenue can't be preserved. The people of Jamaica have been fighting to save their community—and all New York.

"The central issue in the United States is whether we will face the urban crisis, or let our cities die. The people of Jamaica are not going to let their community die.

"To those who say the cities can't be saved, I say, 'Come to Jamaica.'"

We have "come to Jamaica." We have seen the "change at

Jamaica.'' Jamaica, Chelsea, and Coney Island help us to see whether, and how, we can save our neighborhoods—and thus our cities.

Conclusion
BEYOND THE BLOCK

Once upon a time—so the legend goes—there lived a miraculous bird called the phoenix. This winged creature, embodiment of the Egyptian sun god, was fabled to live for 500 years, to be consumed in fire of its own setting, and then to rise in youthful freshness from its own ashes.

It is just possible that a dead or dying city may, like the phoenix, raise itself up from its own ashes. We have seen it happen, or at least begin to happen, in the three city neighborhoods we have been exploring. This rebirth is also starting to take place in many other cities across the land.

Let us first take a look at housing—the most urgent renewal problem of all. Private individuals with the means to do so are responsible for a portion of the revitalization of city neighborhoods.

Restorations such as those we viewed in Chelsea have also taken place in the new-old town houses in the Georgetown area of Washington D.C. Starting in the 1930's, government officials and other professional people in this area began to buy up the quaint 18th and 19th century houses and modernize them.

Or we might turn to Philadelphia, where the lovely old

homes of the Society Hill section have been brought back to their former beauty. Long-time residents and new home purchasers were encouraged to spend the thousands of dollars necessary for renovation because the entire area was being renewed under an elaborate and well-financed plan.

Perhaps not so well known is the home restoration which is going on in a neighborhood that is still largely a black ghetto. Spacious brownstones on tree-lined streets in Brooklyn's Bedford-Stuyvesant are being renovated here in the third largest black community in the country, where massive renewal plans are under way.

Under the leadership of an organization called the Bedford-Stuyvesant Restoration Corporation, eighty banks and nine insurance companies have assured the people of the community of a fund to assist them with mortgages and home refinancing. This aid puts the purchase of a brownstone within the reach of working people with good jobs.

In addition, the corporation offers a home improvement program. Federally funded, this project permits low-cost exterior redecoration of homes on blocks chosen by lottery. The face-lifting involves repairs or replacement of masonry, as well as painting and landscaping, all to be undertaken with local labor.

The residents' sense of involvement and pride in accomplishment is bearing fruit. The renovated blocks have become showcases for the community. Not only are middle-income black families staying in the neighborhood, but they are being joined by a few whites of modest means who like what they see and want to become a part of it.

This kind of rebuilding has been by middle-income people who have money, or the credit to borrow it. They are providing themselves with attractive housing while at the same time collectively making their neighborhood far pleasanter to live in.

What is missing from this picture? It is the poor who have

been displaced from what were once their low-cost shelters. The partitions are down; the units are larger. The net result is more space for fewer people. Because the restoration of old houses is costly, the rentals of apartments in these houses is higher than it was before improvement.

Those who are forced to move to make way for renewal add to the overcrowding in a slum neighborhood elsewhere. The displaced persons are rarely able to remain in the area which is familiar to them.

Middle-class private rehabilitation spells the physical re-birth of an area. It is not, however, human renewal, designed to meet the needs of the poor people who lived in the deteriorated housing. The effect, as we have seen, is often to worsen their lot.

Certain large building developments, made possible through private and government partnership, serve the "middle-third" of the housing market. Middle-income cooper-atives, such as those we visited in Chelsea and Coney Island, have been built in almost all of our large cities. Penn Towne in Philadelphia and Park Town in Cincinnati are examples. And perhaps the largest and most spectacular such effort, opened in 1971, is Co-op City, on the northern fringe of New York City's Borough of the Bronx. Built by the group which put up Penn South in Chelsea and Amalgamated-Warbasse Houses in Coney Island, this project has rehoused 55,000 people in clean, modern skyscraper apartment houses.

Many middle-income urban families might well have re-mained ill-housed or have moved from the city altogether were it not for the partnership of government and the private builder or non-profit housing sponsor.

Another group which is interested in revitalizing its neigh-borhood, and turns to the government for help, is the business community. It, too, finds it can no longer make the needed changes alone.

As we viewed Jamaica's shopping district in process of change, so we might turn to other cities, to see business centers which have been transformed through the combined efforts of businessmen and political leaders.

In a section of Pittsburgh called the Golden Triangle a dramatic transformation took place which was to inspire many urban renewers. Pittsburgh in the 1940's lay under a dark blanket of smog, from the soft coal which heated its houses and powered its steel mills. Forty percent of the business district was blighted or vacant. The assessed value of real estate, which provided one quarter of the tax base of Allegheny County and its school district, was dropping by 18 million dollars a year.

Desperate, as they saw their city spiraling downward, the political and business leaders joined together to turn Pittsburgh around. The Mayor, leading bankers, and industrialists became members of the Pittsburgh Urban Redevelopment Authority in 1946.

Their first goal was to get rid of the unhealthy and ugly air pollution, a job which had been attempted as far back as 1804. The efforts to control the coal smoke had always been fought unsuccessfully. Householders and mill owners used soft coal to fuel their furnaces, cheaply. But the Redevelopment Authority succeeded where all others had failed and soft coal was banned. Then the authority went on, in the 1950's, to rebuild one quarter of the business district. New office towers, hotels, and apartment houses were built by private industry, with government help. Not only was the city's appearance improved, but its financial strength was restored. Citizens of other decaying neighborhoods said "If Pittsburgh could do it, any city can."

In New Haven's Church Street project, an aging commercial area in the heart of the business district was rebuilt in the 1960's, at a cost of 85 million dollars. New office buildings and department stores were brought in, and in addition, streets were made wider, better traffic patterns laid out, and more parking facilities constructed. It all added up to converting a town dating back to colonial times, the horse and buggy era, to a city that today is geared to the motorized age.

For the poor and the dispossessed, however, housing still remains the greatest problem. Even when government aid is offered, neither private builders nor private housing sponsors will undertake to provide decent housing for the bottom economic third of the population. This is why the residents who are relocated when slum clearance starts can seldom return to the neighborhood from which they have been uprooted. Small wonder there are grumblings that renewal programs put "rich people in poor people's houses" or that "urban renewal means Negro removal," when blacks are the slum dwellers.

A partial solution to the housing problems of this "bottom third" is found today in Public Housing. City, state, and federal housing programs are aimed at finding the right locations, workable designs, and a stable mix of economic and racial groups in government built and government operated projects.

In Chelsea, as we have seen, low-income public housing projects have been surrounded by other private and semi-public developments which have improved the neighborhood. The area now contains a mixture of income and racial groups. But where low-income public housing is built as an island in a sea of decay, that island can be overwhelmed, and destroyed.

In St. Louis in 1954, a massive 2,800 unit low-income project was built with federal funds, the Pruitt-Igoe Houses. The project was poorly designed and badly built. The apartments were small, the families for whom they were intended were large. There was inadequate provision for play space, either indoors or out. And too many poor people were herded together, surrounded by other poor people in the neighboring slums.

Pruitt-Igoe Houses was in trouble from the start, so plagued by crime and vandalism that even the desperately poor were reluctant to move in. By 1971 only one-fourth of the apartments were occupied.

Finally, the head of the Housing Authority summed this project up as a "disaster." The Federal Government was urged to tear it down and start all over again. Instead, at a cost of 8 million dollars the development is being drastically altered. The eleven story buildings are being reduced to four and six stories. Some of the buildings are coming down, and town houses and commercial buildings put in their place. Instead of concrete everywhere, two parks are being constructed to make a more livable and balanced community.

There are questions which trouble us about public housing. How can we design these projects so that they do not become instant slums? Do the residents possess the incentives they must have to take care of their buildings? Is ownership, which has worked so well in cooperatives for the middle-income group, a possible solution for low-income groups, too?

And we shall have to find answers, as well, to the question of mix. What balance between low and middle-income housing in a neighborhood will keep the area stable? We know that too great a preponderance of low-income housing may lead to ghettos of the poor, however new the buildings.

Mayor John Lindsay of New York believed in building low-income housing in stable, middle class neighborhoods to prevent the creation of "high-rise ghettos." But the determined opposition of frightened residents of these better communities has prevented much of the housing from being built. Should the efforts at scatter-site housing be continued? Should local opposition be overridden? Should compromises be made? One thing is certain: the housing must be built *somewhere*. Dare we wait for people's hearts and doors to open in welcome?

Another possible approach to the housing of low-income families is still in the experimental stage. Charles J. Urstadt, New York State Commissioner of Housing and Community Renewal, calls it the "scattered-apartment" approach. By its means 2,300 low-income families have by subsidy been placed anonymously among 15,000 middle-income residents in 55 projects. The children of these lower-income families are able to grow up in a middle-income environment. They are not stigmatized; they do not live in low-income buildings; and they need not play in segregated playgrounds.

"In the more than six years of administering this program," the commissioner declares, "I can honestly say I have not had a complaint from or problem with the subsidized tenants, their middle-income neighbors or the building managers."

As we reach the end of our study we find that each problem supposedly solved raises new sets of questions. For example; how much right do the people of a community have to relocate in their own neighborhood after renewal has taken place? Today, in Coney Island and elsewhere, the poor are fighting for the right to remain in the neighborhood in which they have become rooted. They are finding leaders from among their own ranks. Some are also discovering and using their own architects and planners. A new strategy is emerging called Advocacy Planning, in which a given neighborhood determines what kind of community it wants, draws up its own design, and then fights city hall for its creation.

This new kind of planning received a great boost when the Federal Government authorized a Model Cities Program under the Demonstration Cities and Metropolitan Development Act of 1966. The program is designed to help blighted neighborhoods from selected cities in all parts of the country to tackle the whole range of their problems. One hundred and fifty cities are in the program today.

Good housing alone is not a solution to the problems of the

poor, although until recently it was thought to be the hoped-for panacea. Now we know that for the poor to lift themselves from poverty many other facets of their deprivation need to be taken into account and dealt with.

Model Cities is designed to concentrate public and private resources in a comprehensive five year attack on the social and economic problems as well as on the physical aspects of slums. The program aims at raising not only the levels of housing but also of education, health and medical treatment, employment and job training, income, and social services in the model neighborhoods.

It is further specified that residents of the neighborhood and the city as a whole (including labor, business, and other civic groups in the community) should have a hand in identifying problems and planning and carrying out the programs.

Any long-range program that involves government financing depends on continuity of support. When national administrations change, the program which seemed so successful to one set of planners is often thrown out by the new leadership.

Unfortunately, the Model Cities program throughout the country is in deep trouble today. Not only is it, according to a recent presidential task force, "over-regulated" and mired in red tape, but its overriding crisis is lack of funds. It seems that the program, although well conceived, is not receiving the kind of support at the national level needed to make it work locally. Today, the Federal Government is not keeping the promise once made to the Model Cities.

Individual neighborhood groups, in and out of the Model Cities program, are struggling for power and control over the destiny of their neighborhoods. And there is no forward action at all until an answer is found to the question "who speaks for the community?" Unless the people of an area learn to speak with one voice, they are defeated before they start. To be effective, a clear, harmonious chorus must finally emerge from the babel of conflicting shouts. The question still remains, will this be enough? If you fight city hall and win, are you then going to be knocked out by retrenchment on the part of the State or Federal Government? What then, are the odds against the neighborhood determined to renew itself?

These are indeed tough questions for which there are no ready-made answers. First, there are some stubborn facts to be faced. Important among them is that private enterprise is no longer willing or able to build housing in the cities, except for the well-to-do. Government subsidies are needed, not only for the people of low income but for the middle class as well.

Are we putting this subsidized housing in the right places? Or are we simply allowing private developers to build where the profit is—high cost housing in elegant city areas or in the affluent suburbs?

Of one thing we are certain: the problems we have discovered in this study cannot be solved in a piecemeal way. "Block by block" rebuilding is necessary, but it is not enough. Blocks are parts of neighborhoods and neighborhoods are the units that compose a city. Nor can we stop there, for a city belongs to a larger complex—the urban-suburban region.

Planning for the region is therefore part of planning for revitalized cities. Strengthening our city sub-centers, creating satellite cities, designing "New Towns" and other new communities, opening up the wealthy suburbs to provide homes for people of modest income; all of these measures would ease the task of rejuvenating our older cities.

New designs for living, away from the central cities, are at best only a small part of the answer. Land is not endless. Old cities are not expendable. We can no longer move on as we did two hundred or even one hundred years ago. There are just too many of us and there are not enough places to which we can retreat. We can no longer afford a "throw away civilization." Cities, with their exciting potential for a good life, must and can be salvaged.

But where do we begin? Right where we are, in our own backyard and on our own block. We start as lone individuals, and move forward as members of groups working toward a common, mutually agreed upon goal—a better neighborhood in a better city.

Selected Reading List

Abrams, Charles: *The City Is the Frontier.* New York: Harper Colophon Books; 1967

Goodman, Paul and **Percival:** *Communitas: Ways of Livelihood and Means of Life.* New York:Vintage Books; 1960

Harris, Fred R. and **Lindsay, John V.:** *The State of the Cities: Report of the Commission on Cities in the 70's.* New York: Praeger; 1972

Jacobs, Jane: *The Death and Life of Great American Cities.* New York: Vintage Books; 1961

Lowe, Jeanne R.: *Cities in a Race with Time: Progress and Poverty in America's Renewing Cities.* New York: Vintage Books; 1968

Mumford, Lewis: *The Urban Prospect.* New York: Harcourt Brace Jovanovich; 1968

Munzer, Martha E.: *Planning Our Town: An Introduction to City and Regional Planning.* New York: Alfred A. Knopf; 1964 *Pockets of Hope: Studies of Land and People.* New York: Alfred A. Knopf; 1967

Osofsky, Gilbert: *Harlem: The Making of a Ghetto.* New York: Torch Books; 1966

Saarinen, Eliel: *City: Its Growth, Its Decay, Its Future.* Cambridge, Mass.: MIT Press; 1965

Smith, Herbert H.: *The Citizen's Guide to Planning.* West Trenton, New Jersey: Chandler-Davis; 1961

Starr, Roger: *Urban Choices: The City and its Critics.* Baltimore, Md.: Penquin Books; 1967

Tunnard, Christopher and **Henry Hope Reed:** *American Skyline: The Growth and Form of Our Cities and Towns.* New York: Mentor Books; 1956

Udall, Stewart: *Nineteen Seventy-Six: Agenda for Tomorrow.* New York: Harcourt Brace Jovanovich; 1972

Warner, Sam Bass: *Planning for a Nation of Cities.* Cambridge, Mass.: MIT Press; 1966

ABOUT THE AUTHORS

For many years Martha Munzer has successfully combined her work in science and conservation with her interest in young people. She was among the first woman graduates of MIT and subsequently taught chemistry at the Fieldston School in New York for twenty-five years. Following this she joined the Conservation Foundation where she was a staff member for fourteen years. She then lectured and worked with young people at the Wave Hill Center for Environmental Studies. Martha Munzer has written a number of books including *Planning Our Town* and *Pockets of Hope* for Knopf. She lives in Mamaroneck, New York.

Helen Vogel received her B.S. and M.A. degrees from Columbia University. She taught at Eastern New Mexico College and the Walden School in New York. For the past fourteen years she has been teaching adult education courses in the social sciences. Helen Vogel has written another book for Knopf, *Ocean Harvest.* She lives in Scarsdale, New York.